Hernándo Cortés

and the Fall of the Aztecs

Explorers of New Lands

Explorers of New Lands

Hernándo Cortés
and the Fall of the Aztecs

Rachel A. Koestler-Grack

Series Consulting Editor William H. Goetzmann
Jack S. Blanton, Sr. Chair in History and American Studies
University of Texas, Austin

CHELSEA HOUSE
PUBLISHERS
A Haights Cross Communications Company ®

Philadelphia

Cover: A portrait of Hernándo Cortés

CHELSEA HOUSE PUBLISHERS
VP, New Product Development Sally Cheney
Director of Production Kim Shinners
Creative Manager Takeshi Takahashi
Manufacturing Manager Diann Grasse

Staff for HERNÁNDO CORTÉS
Executive Editor Lee Marcott
Editorial Assistant Carla Greenberg
Production Editor Noelle Nardone
Photo Editor Sarah Bloom
Cover and Interior Designer Keith Trego
Layout 21st Century Publishing and Communications, Inc.

A Haights Cross Communications Company ®

www.chelseahouse.com

First Printing

9 8 7 6 5 4 3 2 1

Library of Congress Cataloging-in-Publication

Koestler-Grack, Rachel A., 1973–
   Hernándo Cortés and the fall of the Aztecs/Rachel A. Koestler-Grack.
      p. cm.—(Explorers of new lands)
   Includes bibliographical references and index.
   ISBN 0-7910-8609-7 (hardcover)
   1. Cortés, Hernán, 1485–1547—Juvenile literature. 2. Conquerors—Mexico—
Biography—Juvenile literature. 3. Explorers—Mexico—Biography—Juvenile literature.
4. Explorers—Spain—Biography—Juvenile literature. 5. Mexico—History—Conquest,
1519–1540—Juvenile literature. 6. Mexico—Discovery and exploration—Spanish—
Juvenile literature. I. Title. II. Series.
F1230.C35K64 2005
972'.02'092–dc22
                                                                2005007541

All links and web addresses were checked and verified to be correct at the time of publication.
Because of the dynamic nature of the web, some addresses and links may have changed since
publication and may no longer be valid.

Table of Contents

Introduction

by William H. Goetzmann
Jack S. Blanton, Sr. Chair in History and American Studies
University of Texas, Austin

Explorers have always been adventurers. They were, and still are, people of vision and most of all, people of curiosity. The English poet Rudyard Kipling once described the psychology behind the explorer's curiosity:

"Something hidden. Go and find it. Go and
    look behind the Ranges—
Something lost behind the Ranges. Lost and
    waiting for you. Go!"[1]

Miguel de Cervantes, the heroic author of *Don Quixote*, longed to be an explorer-conquistador. So he wrote a personal letter to King Phillip II of Spain asking to be appointed to lead an expedition to the New World. Phillip II turned down his request. Later, while in prison, Cervantes gained revenge. He wrote the immortal story of *Don Quixote*, a broken-down, half-crazy "Knight of La Mancha" who "explored" Spain with his faithful sidekick, Sancho Panza. His was perhaps the first of a long line of revenge novels—a lampoon of the real explorer-conquistadors.

Most of these explorer-conquistadors, such as Columbus and Cortés, are often regarded as heroes who discovered new worlds and empires. They were courageous, brave and clever, but most of them were also cruel to the native peoples they met. For example, Cortés, with a small band of 500 Spanish conquistadors, wiped out the vast

Aztec Empire. He insulted the Aztecs' gods and tore down their temples. A bit later, far down in South America, Francisco Pizarro and Hernando de Soto did the same to the Inca Empire, which was hidden behind a vast upland desert among Peru's towering mountains. Both tasks seem to be impossible, but these conquistadors not only overcame nature and savage armies, they stole their gold and became rich nobles. More astounding, they converted whole countries and even a continent to Spanish Catholicism. Cathedrals replaced blood-soaked temples, and the people of South and Central America, north to the Mexican border, soon spoke only two languages—Portuguese in Brazil and Spanish in the rest of the countries, even extending through the Southwest United States.

Most of the cathedral building and language changing has been attributed to the vast numbers of Spanish and Portuguese missionaries, but trade with and even enslavement of the natives must have played a great part. Also playing an important part were great missions that were half churches and half farming and ranching communities. They offered protection from enemies and a life of stability for the natives. Clearly vast numbers of natives took to these missions. The missions vied with the cruel native caciques, or rulers, for protection and for a constant food supply. We have to ask ourselves: Did the Spanish conquests raise the natives' standard of living? And did a religion of love appeal more to the natives than ones of sheer terror, where hearts were torn out and bodies were tossed down steep temple stairways as sacrifices that were probably eaten by dogs or other wild beasts? These questions are something to think about as you read the Explorers of New Lands series. They are profound questions even today.

"New Lands" does not only refer to the Western Hemisphere and the Spanish/Portuguese conquests there. Our series should probably begin with the fierce Vikings—Eric the Red, who discovered Greenland in 982, and Leif Ericson, who discovered North America in 1002, followed, probably a year later, by a settler named Bjorni. The Viking sagas (or tales passed down through generations) tell the stories of these men and of Fredis, the first woman discoverer of a New Land. She became a savior of the Viking men when, wielding a broadsword and screaming like a madwoman, she single-handedly routed the native Beothuks who were about to wipe out the earliest Viking settlement in North America that can be identified. The Vikings did not, however, last as long in North America as they did in Greenland and Northern England. The natives of the north were far tougher than the natives of the south and the Caribbean.

Far away, on virtually the other side of the world, traders were making their way east toward China. Persians and Arabs as well as Mongols established a trade route to the Far East via such fabled cities as Samarkand, Bukhara, and Kashgar and across the Hindu Kush and Pamir Mountains to Tibet and beyond. One of our volumes tells the story of Marco Polo, who crossed from Byzantium (later Constantinople) overland along the Silk Road to China and the court of Kublai Khan, the Mongol emperor. This was a crossing over wild deserts and towering mountains, as long as Columbus's Atlantic crossing to the Caribbean. His journey came under less dangerous (no pirates yet) and more comfortable conditions than that of the Polos, Nicolo and Maffeo, who from 1260 to 1269 made their way across these endless wastes while making friends, not enemies, of the fierce Mongols. In 1271, they took along Marco Polo (who was Nicolo's son and Maffeo's nephew). Marco became a great favorite of Kublai Khan and stayed in China till 1292. He even became the ruler of one of Kublai Khan's largest cities, Hangchow.

Before he returned, Marco Polo had learned of many of the Chinese ports, and because of Chinese trade to the west across the Indian Ocean, he knew of East Africa as far as Zanzibar. He also knew of the Spice Islands and Japan. When he returned to his home city of Venice he brought enviable new knowledge with him, about gunpowder, paper and paper money, coal, tea making, and the role of worms that create silk! While captured by Genoese forces, he dictated an account of his amazing adventures, which included vast amounts of new information, not only about China, but about the geography of nearly half of the globe. This is one hallmark of great explorers. How much did they contribute to the world's body of knowledge? These earlier inquisitive explorers were important members of a culture of science that stemmed from world trade and genuine curiosity. For the Polos crossing over deserts, mountains and very dangerous tribal-dominated countries or regions, theirs was a hard-won knowledge. As you read about Marco Polo's travels, try and count the many new things and descriptions he brought to Mediterranean countries.

Besides the Polos, however, there were many Islamic traders who traveled to China, like Ibn Battuta, who came from Morocco in Northwest Africa. An Italian Jewish rabbi-trader, Jacob d'Ancona, made his way via India in 1270 to the great Chinese trading port of Zaitun, where he spent much of his time. Both of these explorer-travelers left extensive reports of their expeditions, which rivaled those of the Polos but were less known, as are the neglected accounts of Roman Catholic friars who entered China, one of whom became bishop of Zaitun.[2]

In 1453, the Turkish Empire cut off the Silk Road to Asia. But Turkey was thwarted when, in 1497 and 1498, the Portuguese captain Vasco da Gama sailed from Lisbon around the tip of Africa, up to Arab-controlled Mozambique, and across the

Indian Ocean to Calicut on the western coast of India. He faced the hostility of Arab traders who virtually dominated Calicut. He took care of this problem on a second voyage in 1502 with 20 ships to safeguard the interests of colonists brought to India by another Portuguese captain, Pedro Álvares Cabral. Da Gama laid siege to Calicut and destroyed a fleet of 29 warships. He secured Calicut for the Portuguese settlers and opened a spice route to the islands of the Indies that made Portugal and Spain rich. Spices were valued nearly as much as gold since without refrigeration, foods would spoil. The spices disguised this, and also made the food taste good. Virtually every culture in the world has some kind of stew. Almost all of them depend on spices. Can you name some spices that come from the faraway Spice Islands?

Of course most Americans have heard of Christopher Columbus, who in 1492 sailed west across the Atlantic for the Indies and China. Instead, on four voyages, he reached Hispaniola (now Haiti and the Dominican Republic), Cuba and Jamaica. He created a vision of a New World, populated by what he misleadingly called Indians.

Conquistadors like the Italian sailing for Portugal, Amerigo Vespucci, followed Columbus and in 1502 reached South America at what is now Brazil. His landing there explains Brazil's Portuguese language origins as well as how America got its name on Renaissance charts drawn on vellum or dried sheepskin.

Meanwhile, the English heard of a Portuguese discovery of marvelous fishing grounds off Labrador (discovered by the Vikings and rediscovered by a mysterious freelance Portuguese sailor named the "Labrador"). They sent John Cabot in 1497 to locate these fishing grounds. He found them, and Newfoundland and Labrador as well. It marked the British discovery of North America.

In this first series there are strange tales of other explorers of new lands—Juan Ponce de León, who sought riches and possibly a fountain of youth (everlasting life) and died in Florida; Francisco Coronado, whose men discovered the Grand Canyon and at Zuñi established what became the heart of the Spanish Southwest before the creation of Santa Fe; and de Soto, who after helping to conquer the Incas, boldly ravaged what is now the

American South and Southeast. He also found that the Indian Mound Builder cultures, centered in Cahokia across the Mississippi from present-day St. Louis, had no gold and did not welcome him. Garcilaso de la Vega, the last Inca, lived to write de Soto's story, called *The Florida of the Inca*—a revenge story to match that of Cervantes, who like Garcilaso de la Vega ended up in the tiny Spanish town of Burgos. The two writers never met. Why was this—especially since Cervantes was the tax collector? Perhaps this was when he was in prison writing *Don Quixote*.

In 1513 Vasco Núñez de Balboa discovered the Pacific Ocean "from a peak in Darien"[3] and was soon beheaded by a rival conquistador. But perhaps the greatest Pacific feat was Ferdinand Magellan's voyage around the world from 1519 to 1522, which he did not survive.

Magellan was a Portuguese who sailed for Spain down the Atlantic and through the Strait of Magellan—a narrow passage to the Pacific. He journeyed across that ocean to the Philippines, where he was killed in a fight with the natives. As a recent biography put it, he had "sailed over the edge of the world."[4] His men continued west, and the *Victoria,* the last of his five ships, worn and battered, reached Spain.

Sir Francis Drake, a privateer and lifelong enemy of Spain, sailed for Queen Elizabeth of England on a secret mission in 1577 to find a passage across the Americas for England. Though he sailed, as he put it, "along the backside of Nueva Espanola"[5] as far north as Alaska perhaps, he found no such passage. He then sailed west around the world to England. He survived to help defeat the huge Spanish Armada sent by Phillip II to take England in 1588. Alas he could not give up his bad habit of privateering, and died of dysentery off Porto Bello, Panama. Drake did not find what he was looking for "beyond the ranges," but it wasn't his curiosity that killed him. He may have been the greatest explorer of them all!

While reading our series of great explorers, think about the many questions that arise in your reading, which I hope inspires you to great deeds.

Notes

1. Rudyard Kipling, "The Explorer" (1898). See Jon Heurtl, *Rudyard Kipling: Selected Poems* (New York: Barnes & Noble Books, 2004), 7.

2. Jacob D'Ancona, David Shelbourne, translator, *The City of Light: The Hidden Journal of the Man Who Entered China Four Years Before Marco Polo* (New York: Citadel Press, 1997).

3. John Keats, "On First Looking Into Chapman's Homer."

4. Laurence Bergreen, *Over the Edge of the World: Magellan's Terrifying Circumnavigation of the Globe* (New York: William Morrow & Company, 2003).

5. See Richard Hakluyt, *Principal Navigations, Voyages, Traffiques and Discoveries of the English Nation*; section on Sir Francis Drake.

Leave None
Without a Wound

As the red sun peaked over the horizon, Hernándo
Cortés pulled himself off the ground. His legs were
so stiff he could barely bend his knees, and the bottoms
of his feet were covered in open blisters. For several
days, he and his Spanish army had been fleeing the
Aztec warriors. Day after day, they fought a bloody

battle. Hundreds of soldiers were slaughtered. But Cortés had the heart of a fearless conqueror. He shook his legs loose of their soreness and walked through the camp. "Rise up, gentlemen," he said. "Take heart. Today, we shall conquer."

On the morning of July 7, 1520, the army formed a marching column. It slowly made its way out of Otumba, a town of friendly natives. The weary army staggered along for three miles. Row by row, the column drew to a sudden halt. The wide eyes of every soldier looked toward the rocky skyline. It seemed as if the entire Aztec army was coming toward them. The soldiers surely believed it was the end for them.

A battle immediately exploded. The sound of clashing swords and whistling sling stones echoed on the plain. "So many natives attacked us," Cortés later wrote, "that we could not see the ground about us."

Cortés felt something warm run down his cheek. He reached his hand up to his face—blood! A sling stone had struck him in the head, leaving a gaping wound. The wound only made him fight harder. He rode his horse around the field, shouting out instructions to his men. "Swords in front of you, gentlemen!" he yelled. "Fight with courage!"

The battle stretched on all day. The bodies of soldiers and natives littered the field. Wounded and fainting, the soldiers almost gave up. Suddenly, Cortés saw the Aztec chief, wearing a rich headpiece made of silver plumes. He carried with him a native banner.

"Now, gentlemen," Cortés shouted with renewed energy, "let us cut our way through them, and leave none of them without a wound!" With a kick to his horse, Cortés charged at the chief and knocked the sacred banner out of his hands. A nearby soldier thrust him with a lance and snatched his silver plumes.

The Spanish continued to ravage the enemy until they retreated. Somehow, the Spaniards found the energy to let out a hearty cheer for their victory. A soldier walked up to Cortés and held out the hat of silver plumes. "This is rightfully yours, Commander," he said.[1]

Hernándo Cortés was a young man during the age of the Spanish conquistadors. In the 1500s, many countries and islands had not yet been

Hernándo Cortés suffered two wounds to his head from sling stones during the Battle of Otumba in July 1520. But the Spanish won the battle, a victory that lifted the soldiers' spirits.

discovered by Europeans. Adventurous sailors set out in small fleets to explore distant lands and claim them for their king.

Of course, these lands already belonged to the natives who lived there. But at the time, the Europeans believed it was their right to take land away from the natives, whom they called "savages." The Europeans did not accept the native way of life. They considered the native culture and way of dress uncivilized. And they thought the natives should become Christians and live like the people in Europe. Many natives died defending their cultures.

Cortés was one of the greatest conquistadors of the sixteenth century. Through incredible hardships, his army defeated the powerful Aztec Empire. His victory secured for Spain the largest kingdom in the New World and gave birth to Spanish America.

Test Your Knowledge

1 Otumba was
  a. a wide river in South America.
  b. a town of hostile Aztec warriors.
  c. a town of natives friendly to the Spaniards.
  d. the name of Cortés's horse.

2 How was Cortés wounded?
  a. By an Aztec spear
  b. By an arrow
  c. By a stray Spanish bullet
  d. By a stone from a sling

3 How did Cortés recognize the Aztec chief?
  a. The chief was the only Aztec with a rifle.
  b. The chief wore a headpiece of silver plumes.
  c. The chief wore a suit of armor.
  d. None of the above.

4 How was Cortés able to rally his weary and wounded troops?
  a. He encouraged them to cut through the enemy toward the chief.
  b. He promised them riches beyond their dreams.
  c. He promised a speedy retreat if they survived the day.
  d. None of the above.

5 How did European cultures of the 1500s view the native peoples of the Americas?

a. As cultural equals

b. As savages, in need of conversion to Christianity

c. As people with a superior way of life

d. None of the above

ANSWERS: 1. c; 2. d; 3. b; 4. a; 5. b

A Reckless
Youth

A young nurse, María de Esteban, gently rocked
Hernándo Cortés in her arms. Only six months
old, he had already been deathly ill several times. María
feared the boy would not make it to his first birthday.
She felt she had to do something to save the poor lad's
life. She wrapped Hernándo in warm blankets and laid

A statue of Hernándo Cortés stands in his birthplace, Medellín, Spain. The town is much the same as it was in his day. Cortés was baptized in the church that is in the left background.

him on the floor near the fire. Then, she walked over to the kitchen table and sat down in front of 12 torn pieces of parchment paper. She carefully took her quill and dipped it in the ink jar. On each scrap of paper, she wrote the name of one of the 12 apostles. As soon as the ink dried, she folded each name in half and dropped it into her winter bonnet.

The baby wiggled in front of the large stone fireplace. María glanced over at the bundle of blankets on the floor. "Be still, precious boy," she whispered. "The angels in heaven will soon be beside you."

She gave the hat a gentle shake and lifted out one piece of paper. "St. Peter," she read. Bold, daring, and outspoken, she remembered—that's the disciple sure to give Hernándo the strength he needs to live. So each day, the young nurse prayed to St. Peter for Hernándo. She pleaded with him to spare the baby's life. Before long, the child recovered. And so at a very young age, Hernándo took St. Peter as his special heavenly advocate and looked to him as a guardian angel. No one imagined this frail child would one day become a fierce conqueror.

Hernán, or Hernándo, Cortés was born in Medellín, Spain, in 1485. His father was Martín

Cortés de Monroy, and his mother was Doña Catalina Pizarro Altamirano. Both of his parents came from ancient, noble families, but they had little money. Like most noble children, however, Hernándo was taken care of by a nurse when he was a baby.

Even though the Cortés family was not wealthy, the people of Medellín had much respect for them. They were good, kind people who earned the love and esteem of everyone. Catalina was honest, strong-minded, and charitable. Martín walked the path of a true Christian, generously giving to anyone in need.

When Hernándo was 14, his parents sent him to study grammar at his uncle's house in the Spanish town of Salamanca. But he stayed for only a short while. Either sick of school or out of money, he returned to Medellín. Hernándo's parents were very disappointed. He was an exceptionally intelligent and clever boy. They had hoped he would someday study law.

But Hernándo was a rowdy and reckless youth. He was forever getting into trouble and starting fights with other boys. With no future at a respectable profession, Hernándo decided to seek out his fortune on the high seas. He had two options. Either he could sail to Naples with Captain Gonzalo Fernández de Córdoba, or go to the Indies with Nicolás de Ovando. He had heard fabulous stories about riches and gold in the Indies. So he chose to sail with Ovando.

While Ovando was getting his fleet ready for departure, Hernándo was still causing mischief. He had met a married woman and made plans to see her in secret. Late one night, he climbed up her garden wall. The wall was poorly cemented and crumbled beneath his feet. The noise awoke the woman's husband. When he came outside and found Hernándo lying in the garden, he went mad with jealousy. He pointed a pistol at the injured young man and threatened to kill him. But before he could pull the trigger, his wife's mother talked him out of it.

Hernándo may have escaped with his life, but his fall left him bedridden. To make matters worse, his injuries turned to fever. He was too sick to sail with Ovando. His great fortune would have to wait.

When he recovered, Hernándo decided to go to Italy. But he only got as far as Valencia, Spain. He stayed in Valencia for a year, barely earning enough money to survive. What he did earn, he spent on wild behavior. Finally, he had wandered enough. He returned to Medellín, again determined to sail for the West Indies. His parents were just happy to see him make a serious decision. They offered to pay for his trip and sent him off with their blessing.

TO THE INDIES!

In 1504, at age 19, Hernándo set sail for the West Indies. Being a daring young man, he went alone— without friend or relative. He had bought passage on the ship of Alonso Quintero. Four other vessels carrying merchandise sailed with him. The voyage went along well from San Lúcar de Barrameda in Spain to Gomer in the Canary Islands.

While the boats were anchored in the Canary Islands, however, Captain Quintero was overcome with greed. During the night, he weighed anchor and sailed away with his ship, with all the crew still on board. Quintero wanted to reach Santo Domingo in the West Indies before the other vessels and sell the goods alone. He had barely set sail when a violent storm rose up at sea. The winds snapped his mast and forced him to return to the Canary Islands.

The other ships had not left yet. Quintero begged for forgiveness and asked his companions to wait while he repaired his ship. Luckily, they agreed. As soon as the repairs were made, the five ships again set sail together.

But Quintero failed to learn his lesson. A favorable wind came up, and he sailed ahead, hoping to outrun the other ships. Again, trouble loomed over him like a curse. His pilot misread their location, and the ship became lost. The sailors were terrified. They had run out of water and were gathering rain to drink. Food was running low, and still no land was in sight. "We're doomed," they cried.

At sunset on Good Friday, a dove flew to the ship and landed on the yardarm. The crew cheered–this was certainly a good omen. On Easter Sunday, the lookout spotted the island of Hispaniola. At first, he was too excited to speak. "Land! Land!" he shouted with tears running down his cheeks.

Cortés, too, breathed a sigh of relief. Like the others, he feared they would be forever lost at sea.

But he refused to show it. This voyage was his first time at sea, and he had promised to face it with the courage of a true seaman.

The pilot recognized the island and set them on the right course. A few days later, the crew anchored at Santo Domingo. The other ships had arrived weeks earlier. In Santo Domingo, Cortés visited a secretary of Ovando, who was now governor of the island. The secretary advised him to become a citizen because he would then get a good piece of land to farm.

But Cortés laughed at him, and said he came for gold, not land. The secretary, though, told him to think it over, reminding him that mining was hard work that rewarded only a lucky few.

Ovando later persuaded Cortés to stay in Santo Domingo for a while. He appointed the young sailor notary of the town council in Azúa—a village Ovando had established. There, Cortés worked as a trader for about six years.

During his stay, Cortés planned to go to Veragua (in Hispaniola) with Diego de Nicuesa. An injury again kept him from setting sail. This time, he had an abscess behind his right knee—an injury that would plague him for the rest of his life. As it turned out, Cortés's injury was a stroke of good luck. Nicuesa's voyage was cursed by hardship and peril. But Cortés would get another chance to hit the high waters.

ADVENTURES IN CUBA

Admiral Don Diego Columbus, governor of the Indies, sent Diego de Velázquez on a conquest to Cuba. By this time, Cortés had acquired a reputation for his skills and intelligence. At Velázquez's request, Cortés accompanied him on the voyage as clerk of the treasurer. As clerk, he would keep a careful account of the royal money.

The Spaniards easily conquered Cuba. Cortés decided to settle in Santiago de Baracoa—the first town on the island. There, he raised cattle, sheep, and horses. But ranching was not enough for Cortés. A greed for gold still lingered inside him. He used the natives as slaves, and forced them to do excruciating labor mining. The natives managed to mine a great deal of gold for Cortés. His wealth earned him much influence and authority with Velázquez.

While in Baracoa, Cortés agreed to marry Catalina Xuárez, a pretty girl from Granada in Spain. But he stalled in going through with the wedding. In anger, Catalina's father went to Velázquez and accused

Spanish Conquistadors

Conquistador is the name given to the soldiers, explorers, and adventurers who brought much of the Americas under Spanish rule during the late fifteenth century and the sixteenth century. The Americas include North America, South America, Central America and the Caribbean. The Spaniards were not mere explorers. They came to rule and take any riches from the land for Spain.

Christopher Columbus's voyage in 1492 marked the start of Spanish expeditions in the New World. Spain first conquered islands in the Caribbean, starting with Hispaniola. Next, Juan Ponce de León conquered Puerto Rico. And Diego de Velázquez took Cuba. In 1519, Hernándo Cortés pushed into central Mexico—the largest Spanish conquest of the time. Most conquistadors were known to be bold, daring, and ruthless. The successful ones, like Cortés, definitely fit that description.

Cortés of many wicked deeds. Velázquez believed the man and arrested Cortés.

Afraid that he wouldn't get a fair trial, Cortés planned an escape. During the night, he broke the padlock of his jail cell, stole a guard's sword and shield, and climbed out a window. In the darkness, he fled to a nearby church for safety. For days, Cortés locked himself in the church, refusing to come out. One day, however, he got caught walking outside the church. Velázquez had him chained in iron shackles and thrown into a strongly sealed vault.

Cortés doubted that he would ever break free. He figured that Velázquez would send him either to Santo Domingo or back to Spain—and worse yet, without any precious gold. Cortés pushed and pulled the shackles around his ankles. His ankles turned bright red and bled from the pressure. Finally, he broke himself loose.

That night, a servant came to deliver his food. Cortés traded clothes with the young man and slipped out a side door unnoticed. He sneaked down to the banks of the Macaniagua River, the river that flows past Baracoa, and rowed off in a small boat.

After the Spaniards conquered Cuba, Cortés settled in Santiago de Baracoa—the first town on the island. But he yearned to be more than a rancher.

But the river current moved in the wrong direction. And it was too strong for Cortés to fight alone. The swirling currents threatened to capsize the boat if he tried to land it. Cortés took off his clothes and tied them in a bundle on his head. He then lowered himself into the water and swam ashore. Once again, he fled to the church.

After Cortés's second escape, Velázquez was impressed with the young man's clever tactics. He sent word to Cortés that he wanted to forget the whole matter. Velázquez invited him to join an expedition to some islands that had rebelled against their Spanish invaders. Wanting peace, Cortés agreed. He quickly married Catalina the same day, just as he had promised to do.

Taking a lance and crossbow, Cortés left at once to join Velázquez. He arrived at the house where Velázquez was staying at a late hour. Seeing Cortés's weapons, Velázquez became frightened. He thought perhaps Cortés planned to take revenge on him.

Cortés assured him that he had not come to fight and asked Velázquez to take his hand in friendship. The two men shook hands. In this way, Cortés regained respect and honor with Velázquez.

Velázquez marveled at the young man's determination and vigor. He secretly thought that Cortés was destined for great things.

Test Your Knowledge

1 Which saint did Cortés's nurse credit with saving him?

a. St. Bartholomew

b. St. Paul

c. St. Peter

d. St. Anthony

2 Which of the following best characterizes Cortés's youth?

a. Studious and focused

b. Wild and reckless

c. Devoutly religious

d. None of the above

3 Why did Cortés have to delay his first trip to sea?

a. He suffered with pneumonia.

b. His parents bribed him to stay close to home.

c. He wanted to marry a local girl.

d. He was injured in a fall while pursuing an adulterous relationship.

4 What delayed the arrival of Cortés at Santo Domingo?

a. The ship he was on was attacked by pirates.

b. There was a mutiny aboard Cortés's ship.

c. One captain's greedy scheme to get ahead of the fleet got him lost.

d. None of the above.

5 What impressed Velázquez most about the young Cortés?

a. The clever ways Cortés twice managed to escape jail

b. The way Cortés wielded a sword

c. The way Cortés managed the royal funds in his control

d. None of the above

ANSWERS: 1. c; 2. b; 3. d; 4. c; 5. a

We Shall Conquer

Diego de Velázquez sent expeditions west toward present-day Mexico in 1517 and 1518. Juan de Grijalva, the leader of the second expedition, brought back reports of a mighty kingdom in the center of the land—the Aztec Empire.

Intrigued, Velázquez wanted to learn more about this awesome empire. But leading such an expedition would take a man with an iron will and ruthless determination. He must be brave to the point of insanity. Not to mention, he had to find someone willing to pay for the voyage himself. Velázquez was an incredibly stingy governor. Only one name came to Velázquez's mind. He ordered his officers to get him Hernándo Cortés.

PREPARING THE FLEET

Governor Velázquez set up two financial backers for Cortés. One was the governor's secretary, Andrés de Duero. The other was the king's accountant, Amador de Lares. Cortés was appointed captain-general of the whole fleet, with abounding powers. In return, Cortés agreed to divide any gold, silver, and jewels that became his share with the other three men. Velázquez claimed his desire was to conquer and settle the land for the king of Spain. But secretly, he was only interested in trade and riches.

Before the ink on the contract was even dry, Velázquez had second thoughts about making

(continued on page 29)

Early Mexican Conquests

The conquest of Mexico came in two stages. The first stage established permanent settlements in the Caribbean Sea and outposts on the island of Cuba. With these towns, the Spaniards were able to explore the Mexican mainland and Central America, knowing that they could quickly return to their outposts if necessary. The second stage was actually conquering the mainland.

In the early 1500s, the first governor of Cuba—Diego de Velázquez—sponsored three expeditions to explore the Gulf of Mexico. The Spanish navigator and conqueror Francisco Hernández de Córdoba led the first trip. Córdoba set sail from Cuba in 1517, discovered what he believed to be an island, and called it Yucatán. Here, he found a much more advanced culture than that of the Caribbean natives. These people were the Mayas. They wore cotton garments, lived in stone houses, and built cities. They farmed large fields of maize, or corn. Córdoba believed that the Mayas also had gold and silver. Near Champoton, the Spanish sailors went ashore for water. Maya warriors suddenly attacked them. During a major battle, more than half of the

Spanish sailors were killed. Córdoba, too, was injured. He immediately returned to Velázquez to report his discovery. He died shortly after from his wounds. But his expedition sparked further interest in Mexico.

In 1518, Velázquez organized another expedition. This time, he chose his nephew Juan de Grijalva as the commander. Grijalva returned to Champoton to avenge Córdoba's defeat. After three days of fierce fighting, the Mayas retreated. Grijalva and his men continued to explore the Gulf Coast. Eventually, they encountered friendly Mayas. Grijalva confirmed Córdoba's report of gold; nearly everything the natives traded with him was in some ways made of gold.

Grijalva explored the coast all the way to the Pánuco River, near Tampico. There, the native leaders told Grijalva about a powerful lake kingdom to the west. Although they did not know it at the time, the Spanish had reached the outer edges of the Aztec Empire. Grijalva brought this news back to Velázquez, telling him that the natives said the Aztecs were rich and powerful. The following year, Cortés embarked on his epic conquest.

The ancient Mayan ruins of Tikal rise above the treeline. When Spanish explorers first reached the Yucatán Peninsula of Mexico, the natives they encountered were the Maya.

(continued from page 25)

Cortés commander of the expedition. Velázquez constantly feared that his men were trying to cheat him. Velázquez worried that Cortés might take revenge on him because of their rocky past.

Realizing the governor might change his mind, Cortés did not waste any time. He went to work equipping his fleet. He rounded up guns, powder, crossbows—any weapons he could find. He supplied arms and armor for all the crew. He stocked all kinds of items that he would use for bartering and trade. Above all, Cortés wanted the proper manpower for his expedition. He employed 300 officers and men, but added another 200 before the fleet left Cuba. He also brought along 200 Cuban natives as servants and carriers. Cortés ordered hundreds of pounds of food stores to be loaded. He bought live pigs and turkeys, salt pork, cornbread, wine, oil, chickpeas, maize, sugar, and barrels of water.

His most bizarre request was for 16 horses. Horses were not native to Cuba. They had to be brought over from Spain. Bringing a horse across the ocean was difficult work, and many of the animals died en route. For this reason, horses were very expensive, and he could only manage to gather

16 of them. Cortés's decision turned out to be a stroke of genius. The horses became the expedition's strong point and hope of survival. Not only would they prove invaluable in battle, but they would also have a psychological effect on the natives. To the Aztecs, the horses would look like creatures from myths and tales. The sight of these strange and powerful animals was sure to strike fear in the hearts of the natives.

In outfitting his fleet, Cortés spent all of his own money and went into incredible debt. He wanted to make sure his expedition would be the best-equipped one ever to sail to Mexico. He was extremely careful and thorough in all his preparations. When he would land in Mexico, he would be bankrupt. But he knew he would have all the necessities of war and survival.

Cortés appointed 10 captains and divided his crew into 11 armies. He gave a company of men to each captain, keeping a headquarter company for himself. Each of Cortés's captains was fearless and independent, and like him, most of them were in their early to mid-30s. Captain Alonso de Avila was one of Grijalva's men, and Francisco de Montejo was the father of the future conqueror of the Yucatán. He also chose Juan de Escalante, Juan Velázquez de León, Cristóbal de Olid, and a man called Escobar. As his most trusted advisor, Cortés chose 24-year-old Gonzalo de Sandoval. Sandoval had a strong and commanding personality. He was uncommonly brave, and although shorter than most men, he was sturdy and muscular.

After assembling his fleet as quickly as possible, Cortés thought it best to set sail immediately. The agreement had been signed on October 23, 1518, and the commander planned to set sail the morning of November 18—less than four weeks later. On the evening of November 17, Cortés ordered his officers to board the ships at nightfall. Meanwhile, he kept the governor busy late into the night. With everything ready, Cortés invited Velázquez down to the port in Santiago the following morning. He asked him to give the crew his blessing before they set sail.

As it turned out, Cortés acted in the nick of time. No sooner had the fleet weighed anchor then the governor panicked. By the time Cortés reached Trinidad, two officers had orders to arrest him as a

The fleet of Cortés, bound for Mexico, sails out of the harbor of Santiago, Cuba. Just after the fleet left, Governor Diego de Velázquez had second thoughts about having Cortés lead the mission and ordered him stopped.

rebel and stop the ships. Cortés used his gift of smooth speech to win the messengers over to his side. He promised to reward them with a share of the coming riches. He also warned them that if they tried to arrest him, the crew might get out of hand.

After 10 days, the fleet moved on to Havana—a town at the opposite end of Cuba. Cortés wanted to be as far away from Velázquez's hand as he could get while he made his final preparations. Velázquez was furious at being outsmarted by Cortés and sent his chief representative to carry out the orders his messengers had failed to do. In a matter of minutes, Cortés again talked his way out of arrest. The governor's representative sent a letter back, assuring him that Cortés was loyal and respectable. He certainly would never turn against Velázquez.

Finally, the expedition was ready to embark. Cortés called his crews onto the beach. "We are engaging in a just and good war which will bring us fame . . ." he said in a strong, confident voice. "If you do not abandon me, as I shall not abandon you, I shall make you in a very short time the richest of all men who have ever crossed the seas . . ."[2] With more than 500 men in 11 small ships, the fleet set sail around February 10, 1519. The crewmen hoisted banners decorated with the royal coat of arms and a cross on each side. These banners, waving majestically in the breeze, hailed the fleet's purpose. *"Comrades, let us follow the sign of the holy cross with true faith, and through it, we shall conquer."*[3]

Test Your Knowledge

1 How did Diego de Velázquez fund Cortés's expedition to the Aztec Empire?
   a. He put up all the money himself.
   b. He found two prominent backers.
   c. He persuaded the pope to fund the expedition.
   d. None of the above.

2 Why was it unusual for Cortés to order horses for his expedition?
   a. Horses could not be expected to navigate the jungle paths.
   b. It was illegal to export horses from Spain.
   c. It was difficult and expensive to transport horses by sea.
   d. None of the above.

3 Who was Gonzalo de Sandoval?
   a. A spy whom Velázquez placed among Cortés's crew
   b. A wily trader Cortés believed could negotiate with the Aztecs
   c. A priest sent on the expedition by the Catholic Church
   d. A trusted advisor to Cortés, and a man known for his bravery

4 Why did Velázquez try twice to have Cortés arrested?

   a. Velázquez was a suspicious man and distrusted the young explorer.

   b. Velázquez discovered that Cortés had stolen church funds.

   c. Velázquez had lost the financial support of his backers.

   d. None of the above.

5 How did Cortés twice avoid arrest?

   a. He killed the messengers sent by Velázquez.

   b. He sailed at night before the messengers could catch him.

   c. He talked his way out of trouble.

   d. None of the above.

ANSWERS: 1. b; 2. c; 3. d; 4. a; 5. c

The Conquest Begins

The fleet endured a choppy voyage to Mexico. The small vessels were tossed on the waves of a Caribbean storm. The forceful winds blew the ships in every direction, separating the fleet. One ship was lost for several weeks. Most of the ships took four days to cross 200 miles from Havana to the Yucatán.

They finally landed near their destination, Cozumel.

Cortés and his flagship had been blown off course. But it managed to catch up with the other ships several days later. Since the expedition began, the flagship had sailed off course twice. Cortés's fierce command brought the vessel back from danger. But he was also angry. When the ship landed at Cozumel, he ordered the pilot put in irons, or shackles. He needed to prove his authority to the crewmen to gain their respect. In order for his mission to be successful, he would have to maintain control over his men.

Upon arriving at Cozumel, Cortés received some alarming news. One of his men, Pedro de Alvarado, had taken command and took rash action. As the Spanish ships approached, Alvarado saw the natives abandon their village and run into the woods. He encouraged the other sailors to go ashore and forage through the empty village, stealing anything of value they could find.

Cortés was appalled. This act could have put the expedition in serious danger. Cortés did not intend to make a quick battle and retreat. He had

Hernándo Cortés and his men landing near Cozumel, Mexico, in 1519. While in Cozumel, Cortés found two Spaniards who had been shipwrecked earlier and taken as slaves by the natives. One of them was freed to Cortés and became a useful interpreter.

a well-planned strategy that was to be carried out carefully. The natives were not to be treated like out-right savages. Cortés hoped to make as many allies as he could. He understood that Mexico was a large land with many natives. There was no way he could simply march through the jungle and defeat every village he encountered. His weapons and supplies were limited. He would have to act cautiously, making friends whenever he could. He hoped some of these natives would help his men find food and water along the way. Immediately, Cortés found one of the natives and treated him with kindness. He offered the man many gifts in exchange for the items his men had stolen. Cortés's diplomacy worked perfectly. Peace was made, and the native even agreed to take Cortés back to his village.

While in Cozumel, Cortés received a remarkable piece of luck. His interpreter learned that a nearby village had a couple of Spanish slaves. The Spaniards had been shipwrecked on an earlier expe-dition. Amazingly, one of the men—Jerónimo de Aguilar—showed up at Cortés's village. He dropped to his knees before the commander. At first, Cortés was confused, because the man looked like a native.

Aguilar looked tattered. He wore an old sandal on one foot and a ragged cloak over his shoulders. As soon as the man began to speak, however, Cortés knew he was a Spaniard.

"Eight years ago, 15 men and two women were left stranded in this land," he explained. "All are dead now, except myself and another man—Gonzalo Guerrero."

Suddenly, tears streamed out of his eyes. "An army of natives captured some of us and put us in cages." He paused for a moment. "They planned to use us as a sacrifice to their god, but we escaped."

The survivors found their way to a friendly village. There, they worked as common slaves. When the village leader, or cacique, heard about Cortés's fleet, he agreed to free the two men. Guerrero, though, chose to stay. He had accepted the culture, taken a native bride, and had three pretty children.

"I am asking you to take me with you," Aguilar pleaded.

Cortés was thrilled and took Aguilar's hands in his own. Aguilar was fluent in several Maya dialects. He would be a useful interpreter in the weeks ahead. "You are much needed on this expedition," Cortés told him. "It is truly a miracle that God has brought you to us." [4]

Before leaving Cozumel, Cortés had one more task. In the name of Christianity, he threw down every religious idol of the native village. The interpreter gently explained that these images were not gods, but evil figures that would lead their souls to hell. He then told the natives about Jesus Christ and the Christian religion. Cortés gave the natives a cross and a statue of the Virgin Mary to put up in place of the idols. Cortés would go through this process in every village he visited. Some natives accepted his words and promised to obey him. Others turned hostile and drove him out of their villages.

THE FIRST BATTLE

The ships crawled along the coast, hugging the shoreline as closely as they could. After a 10-day journey, the fleet finally dropped anchor at the mouth of the Río Grijalva. This river flows through the city of Villahermosa, capital of the Tabasco territory. Some of the crew rowed ashore in small boats.

Cortés was disappointed to find that the Tabascans were hostile. According to Francisco Hernández de

Córdoba and Juan de Grijalva, these people were friendly. But the Spaniards had called them cowards, which the Tabascans were eager to prove wrong. Cortés's army was about to get its first taste of action.

When his men landed, the whole bank was thick with native warriors. They carried spears, sounded trumpets, and beat drums. Aguilar tried to calm them down. He asked if the men could land, get water, and talk to them about God. He added that if they attacked the Spanish, the soldiers would have to fight back in self-defense. If any of the natives were killed, it would be their fault and not the soldiers'. One man wrote, "Cortés endeavored to offer them peace one, two and many times before making war on them or invading their lands and taking their towns."[5]

Cortés's peace talk failed. The natives began attacking the soldiers with bows and arrows. Cortés and his immediate crew were quickly surrounded. They were saved just in time by the tardy arrival of another army force. By nightfall, the Spanish forces had captured the small town of Potonchán. The skirmish continued the next day, and another small village was taken.

Hernándo the Hidalgo

In 711, the Muslims invaded the Iberian Peninsula, which includes Portugal and present-day Spain. This invasion began a 700-year struggle for control of the peninsula. The war was called the Reconquista—a religious crusade against the Moors, which the Muslims were called, to reconquer Spain. The Reconquista had two main purposes: to bring Christianity back to the land and to make a royal claim to the land for the Spanish crown. Without these two claims, the fight would lack any moral or legal authority. This practice eventually became the system for conquistadors in the New World.

Out of the Reconquista came a new type of warrior—the hidalgo. A hidalgo devoted his life to defending Spain. He was not a nobleman or a lord. But instead, he was more of a vagabond knight. A hidalgo could do the impossible through sheer physical courage and a valiant will. He lived by a strict code of honor. Hidalgos respected men who won riches by violent force rather than hard work. The concept of the hidalgo spread throughout all areas of society and became an ideal for men. This ideal—to conquer by force—later became the basic goal of conquistadors like Hernándo Cortés.

The third day, March 25, brought the deciding battle. The Tabascans had gotten help from the important town of Cintla, which was about 12 miles inland. Cortés realized that he must plan a careful engagement if he expected to win. He strategically picked his position on a level plain between the town and the sea. He ordered some men back to the ships to bring six cannons and thirteen horses.

The Spanish soldiers marched onto the field in rows. They pointed their long, steel-tipped ashwood lances to the sky. As they ran into battle, they looked like an "iron cornfield."

The entire savannah was covered with native warriors. Their faces were painted black and white, and they wore great feather headdresses. They carried bows and arrows, spears and shields, and slings. "They rushed on us like mad dogs and completely surrounded us," one soldier remembered, "discharging such a rain of arrows, darts, and stones upon us that more than 70 of our men were wounded in the first attack."[6]

Cortés put himself in charge of the cavalry unit. At first, he had trouble riding through the marshy terrain at the rear of the enemy. But his late arrival made the effect all the more powerful. The Mayas were shocked at the sight of these half-animal, half-human creatures. They stood paralyzed in fear as hoofs pounded around them. Both armies dashed at the enemy, cutting the natives down with their glittering swords. The Mayas suffered a terrible defeat at the Battle of Cintla.

The next day, a group of about 40 natives came to Cortés to discuss peace. Cortés had already planned a show for his defeated enemies. He ordered out his largest cannon and two strong horses. As he spoke, he gave a signal for the cannon to be fired. The thundering bang of the gun and the whistle of the ball through the air terrified the natives.

"The cannons are still angry from being attacked," Cortés claimed.

Then, the sailors brought out the two horses whinnying and stomping. Again, the natives froze in horror. "The horses, too, are restless," Cortés added.

The commander explained that the guns and horses would settle down now that the natives wanted to make peace. Cortés claimed the new land in the name of the king of Spain. He picked up his sword and struck a cottonwood tree three times.

y epolínhą mexica

Drawings show encounters between the Spanish and the natives in Mexico. In one, a Spaniard with feathers in his hat talks to two natives carrying shields. In another, a Spaniard leads a line of natives.

"We will defend the king's right with our very lives!" he shouted.[7] Turning to the natives, he invited them to join the king as his vassals.

For the most part, Cortés was mild and gracious with the natives. After much debate, Spain and Tabasco finally forged a treaty. The caciques of

Tabasco offered Cortés some objects made of gold as a symbol of their loyalty. The first conquest of Mexico had been made.

Cortés learned that there was little gold in this area. But the natives told him there was much more to be found in the direction of the setting sun. The Mayas pointed their fingers west. Great riches lie in the kingdom of Colhúa, they told him.

Aguilar turned to Cortés. "Mexico," he replied.

The Spanish conquistadors looked toward the sunset. They felt excitement and gloom. The marvelous land they had heard about was within reach. But their journey and warfare had only begun.

Test Your Knowledge

1 Why did Cortés order his pilot thrown in irons at Cozumel?

a. He learned that the pilot was a Portuguese spy.

b. He needed to reaffirm his authority after his ship had become lost.

c. The pilot had been stealing extra rations of food and water.

d. The pilot had attempted to organize a mutiny against Cortés.

2 In what way was the rescue of Jerónimo de Aguilar lucky for Cortés?

a. Aguilar had a map to the Aztec capital.

b. Aguilar knew where much gold and treasure were hidden.

c. Aguilar could speak Mayan and would be valuable as a translator.

d. None of the above.

3 Why did Cortés destroy the native idols at Cozumel?

a. He wanted to convince the natives of his military strength.

b. He wanted the natives to shun their gods in favor of Christianity.

c. He thought that the native idols contained hidden gold.

d. None of the above.

4 Why were the Tabascans hostile to Cortés?

a. The Spaniards had insulted them by calling them cowards.

b. The Tabascans were loyal to the Portuguese.

c. The Tabascans had a long history of being hostile to outsiders.

d. None of the above.

5 What happened at the Battle of Cintla?

a. Cortés and his men were briefly surrounded.

b. Cortés used his superior weapons and horsemen to defeat the Mayans.

c. Cortés made his first conquest for Spain in Mexico.

d. All of the above.

ANSWERS: 1. b; 2. c; 3. b; 4. a; 5. d

Moctezuma

T he ships set sail from Tabasco. They moved along the coast past the town of Coatzacoalcos and the landmarks from Grijalva's voyage. After covering about 250 miles, the fleet finally cast anchor at San Juan de Ulúa.

As they landed, Captain Portocarrero slapped Cortés on the back. "You are looking on rich lands," he said. "May you know how to govern them well!"[8]

In a way, Portocarrero let the "cat out of the bag." His comment revealed a secret plot by Cortés and his close companions. Portocarrero used the word "govern." Officially, the governor of Cuba sent Cortés. Therefore, any land that the explorer seized would become part of Velázquez's domain. From the very beginning, Cortés had planned to be the governor of these great lands.

In order to make his plan work, the crew members would have to transfer their loyalty from Velázquez to King Charles I of Spain (who became Holy Roman Emperor Charles V in 1519). Spain was far away, and the emperor had no idea what was going on in Mexico. But Charles could hardly refuse Cortés if the commander could prove his conquest a success, send Charles a good deal of treasure, and promise that there would be more. It mattered little to the emperor who governed Mexico, as long as his treasury was being filled.

To capture Charles's interest, Cortés sent him a message. He wrote, "In our judgment, it is entirely possible that this country has everything which existed in the land from which Solomon is said to have brought gold for the temple." How intrigued the king must have been at such a lavish picture of this land.

But Cortés did not stop there. He was out for it all. He also sent another message—one that would sever all friendly ties between him and Velázquez. "We have good cause to fear him, for we have seen what he has done in Cuba," Cortés complained. "He renders justice as he pleases, punishing those whom he chooses. . . . He is involved with dishonest men, seeking always his own advantage." He concluded his message by pleading, "We pray you not to grant him governorship of this land."[9]

It was ironic that Cortés accused Velázquez of self-ishness. In fact, Cortés's greed for this land "flowing with milk and honey" had all but taken control of him. But his persuasion worked on the emperor. His men appointed Cortés as governor, captain-general, and chief justice of a new Spanish town named Villa Rica de Vera Cruz. Today, it is known as

Old Veracruz, just 20 miles north of new Veracruz. The town had shifted south to take advantage of a better harbor, and it quickly grew in population. Cortés laid the first stones with his own hands.

Cortés had now achieved independence for his mission. By wooing his crew, he earned the right to take one-fifth of any treasure that was found.

A KINGDOM DIVIDED

Taking care of diplomatic issues made for some much-needed peaceful weeks on the coast. Cortés had built his town near Cempoala, in the Totonac territory. The natives of this area were called Cempoalans. Cortés made routine marches throughout the country, visiting native towns and throwing down their idols.

He also discovered a cruel and gruesome practice of the natives. They offered human sacrifices to their gods. In the ceremony, the victim was laid across a saddle-shaped stone. The priest stabbed a knife into the left side of the victim's chest, just under the breast. He then yanked the knife downward, making a gaping cut through the body. He reached inside and pulled out the still-beating heart.

The coast of Cempoala, Mexico. Cortés landed nearby and established the town of Villa Rica de Vera Cruz. At Cempoala, Cortés first heard about Moctezuma II, the leader of the Aztec Empire.

In Aztec culture, to be a victim of sacrifice was actually an honor. Each native was ready for death at any moment. "Your turn today, my turn tomorrow," they would say.[10] Anyone could be a tribute sacrifice—male, female, adult, child, or infant. Cortés abhorred such tributes and vowed to end this wicked behavior.

At the same time, Cortés was pleased with the extravagant gifts the Cempoalans brought to him. They brought fine items made from gold and silver. Their gifts were much more impressive than the gold and silver disks and gold bracelets of the Mayas at Cozumel.

Here at Cempoala, Cortés first heard the name Moctezuma II, ruler of the Aztecs. The Totonacs were like vassals to the Aztecs. Upon hearing of the newcomers, the Totonac leaders ordered paintings of Cortés, his ships, officers, captains, and even the horses to send to Tenochtitlán—the great capital city of the Aztec Empire. This way, their lord could see what these white men looked like.

Cortés was delighted to learn that the Totonacs hated their overlords. Each year, Moctezuma's officers would take away many of their sons and daughters for sacrifice. The Totonacs despised him for his cruelty, yet feared him. The fact that Moctezuma had enemies within the kingdom would serve Cortés's purpose nicely. He remembered the words of the apostle Matthew, "Any kingdom divided against itself is laid waste." It is easier to conquer a divided kingdom than a united one.

The Aztecs offered human sacrifices to their gods, as seen here in an Aztec manuscript. The sacrifices horrified Cortés, who vowed to end the practice.

Soon, Cortés got a chance to make an impression on the rebel Totanacs. While he was talking to a Cempoalan cacique, he saw 20 Aztec men approaching the village. They appeared to be important officials. The cacique and his friends trembled in fear. Cortés asked them why they were so scared.

They explained that the Aztec men were Moctezuma's tribute collectors. The cacique and his friends feared that if the Aztecs saw them talking to Cortés, Moctezuma would bring his wrath down on them.

Cortés assured them not to worry. He ordered his soldiers to seize Moctezuma's men, beat them, tie them to poles, and carry them off to a nearby house. He assigned several soldiers to guard the house.

The arrest of the Aztecs was only half of Cortés's plan. In the middle of the night, when the Cempoalans were asleep, Cortés told his men to untie two of the prisoners and bring them to his ship. He explained to the two confused Aztecs that it was all a misunderstanding.

Cortés claimed that the Cempoalans were going to kill the Aztecs so he arrested them to save their lives. He pledged friendship and devotion to Moctezuma. Cortés promised not to harm the other prisoners. He fed the two Aztecs a large meal. After they had eaten, Cortés's men rowed them back to shore and landed in a safe and hidden spot. They hurried back to Tenochtitlán with the message from the Spaniards.

The next morning, the Cempoalans were horrified to see that the two Aztecs had escaped. "They're on the way back to Moctezuma," the Cempoalans gasped, fearing what the leader would do when he heard how his messengers were treated.

The natives immediately called a council. Some Cempoalans thought they should send a tribute at

Beware the Espantos!

The Aztec ruler Moctezuma II was superstitious. He studied witchcraft, and a series of evil omens had him nervous. The strange happenings began in 1509. The ruler of Nezahualpilli, a neighboring Aztec town, sent messengers to Moctezuma. His wise men had predicted the fall of the Aztec Empire. At first, Moctezuma did not believe them. His wise men said they saw no such visions.

But weird events kept happening. Tongues of flames sparked in the sky. A fire suddenly broke out in the temple of Huitzilopochtli. People rushed in with buckets of water to put out the flames. But the more water they poured on it, the greater the fire raged. One day, a storm rose up on the lake. The water on the lake appeared as if it was boiling. At night, the Aztecs could hear voices crying. One woman cried, "My children, let us flee! My children, where can we hide ourselves?"

once. He could plead for mercy and explain that it was the Spaniards' fault. Others argued that they had been victims of Moctezuma's cruelty long enough and that it was time to fight back. Perhaps

Some Aztec fishermen brought to the emperor the strangest sign of all. While out on the lake, they discovered a dark-colored bird. On top of its head was a small mirror. When Moctezuma looked into the mirror he saw a vision. He saw Aztec warriors fighting men who rode on animals that looked like a deer. These espantos, or frights, made the Aztecs jittery. They wondered what the gods had planned for them. Today, many Mexican natives still believe in espantos and blame them for illnesses.

When Cortés arrived in Mexico, the Aztecs thought the prophecy was coming true. The Aztecs must have been downhearted. They certainly could not fight the gods. This mentality probably helped Cortés take over Tenochtitlán so easily at first. But the Aztecs managed to pull themselves together, and conquer their superstitions. Perhaps they waited too long to react. Maybe it was their own beliefs that kept them from winning the war.

the Spanish soldiers would help them. In the end, the Cempoalans decided to rise up and rebel against Moctezuma. They asked Cortés to be their leader.

Cortés agreed to help them, saying that their friendship was more valuable to him than Moctezuma's. He asked how many of their warriors they could find. The cacique replied that they could bring 100,000. Cortés was thrilled at the bursting size of his new army. By his shrewd actions, Cortés both won Moctezuma's trust—which would get him inside the great city—and the support of the natives in a revolt.

Messengers ran at once to all the surrounding towns and villages. They praised the Spanish soldiers, and declared an open war against Moctezuma. Cortés now had the strength and resistance he needed to wage war against the powerful Aztec ruler.

Test Your Knowledge

1 What secret plot did Cortés and his close companions share?

   a. Cortés planned to kill Velázquez and take control of Cuba.

   b. Cortés planned to become governor of any lands he conquered.

   c. Cortés planned to cheat King Charles of Spain out of any gold.

   d. None of the above.

2 How did the Aztec natives perform their human sacrifices?

   a. They cut out the victim's beating heart with a knife.

   b. They let venomous snakes bite the sacrifice.

   c. They poisoned the sacrifice with toxic herbs.

   d. They threw the victim into the mouth of a volcano.

3 Why was Cortés pleased that the Totonac leaders disliked Moctezuma?

   a. He hoped to raise an army of discontent natives to fight the Aztecs.

   b. He understood the value of forging new alliances.

   c. He knew that a divided nation would be easier for him to defeat.

   d. All of the above.

4 How did Cortés use the dislike between the Cempoalan and Aztec people to his advantage?

a. He murdered the Aztec tribute-collectors and blamed the Cempoalans.

b. He captured some Aztec tribute collectors, assured them of his devotion to Moctezuma. then secretly released them.

c. He burned a Cempoalan village and blamed the Aztecs.

d. None of the above.

5 How many men did the Cempoalans pledge to Cortés?

a. 1,000

b. 5,000

c. 10,000

d. 100,000

ANSWERS: 1. b; 2. a; 3. d 4. b; 5. d

March to Tenochtitlán

After three months in Villa Rica, Cortés was in the mood to get a look at Moctezuma. But he first had to stamp out a conspiracy within his own ranks. Some of the men had planned to steal a ship, sail to Cuba, and tell Velázquez what Cortés was doing. Cortés had the four leaders of the rebellion brought before him for punishment. He sentenced two of them to be hanged, one flogged—or severely whipped—and one to have his feet cut off. As he signed the sentence, Cortés breathed a heavy sigh and uttered the famous words of the Roman emperor Nero: "It would be better not to know how to write, for one would then be unable to confirm death sentences." [11] Once again, Cortés proved that he was an unbreakable leader who refused to be challenged.

Cortés put the finishing touches on the preparations for the march to Tenochtitlán. He was also planning a final, dramatic finish before leaving the coast. His final action was a real gamble, so much so that he kept it a secret from most of the officers and crew. When all was ready for the march, Cortés destroyed the fleet. He ordered the ship masters to strip out the guns, provisions, anchors, cables, sails, and any other items of use. Some of the ships he scuttled; the scuttle hatch in the hull of the ship opened to let the water in. He bored holes into the hulls of the other ships.

When the soldiers heard of the news, they flew into a rage. How could they ever escape if the natives forced them to retreat?

Just before the march to Tenochtitlán, Cortés scuttled his ships, destroying his fleet. He wanted to prevent soldiers from deserting the army and fleeing back to the coast.

"Does he want to send us to the slaughterhouse?" one sailor yelled.

"You will now only have God to look to for help," Cortés replied. "You must rely on your own good swords and stout hearts." [12]

Another reason Cortés sunk the fleet was so that no soldier would think of deserting the army and running back to the coast. Destroying the fleet also freed up all the sailors to join the soldiers on land, although most of them bucked at the chore.

The entire company of Spaniards—about 500 in all—began their march inland on August 16, 1519. The route Cortés took from Villa Rica to Tenochtitlán was a difficult one. He could have taken a southern route through present-day Orizaba, instead of the northern path through Jalapa. The southern terrain would have been easier on his men and horses. He chose the roundabout way because the Totonacs told him the Tlaxcalans of the northern region would welcome the Spaniards. As it turned out, the Totonacs were grossly mistaken in their judgment of the Tlaxcalans.

The Tlaxcalans consisted of five large tribes. They were proud warriors and heavily armed. And they also had a hatred for their Aztec neighbors. On the downside, they kept themselves apart from the outside world. They knew nothing about the Spanish and their plan to take down the Aztecs.

When the Tlaxcalans saw an armed force moving through their land, they had a hard time believing the group was friendly. Cortés repeatedly sent messages to Chief Xicotenga explaining that the soldiers came in peace and only wished to pass through his country on their way to Tenochtitlán.

But the Tlaxcalans feared the Aztecs and were slow to trust. What if this army was an ally of Moctezuma's? They thought Cortés's men planned to attack them from the east while the Aztecs invaded from the west.

WAR WITH TLAXCALA

The Tlaxcalans fought the Spaniards every step of the way. Cortés's army was ambushed at mountain passes. The Tlaxcalan warriors hurled rocks and threw spears. The soldiers were tormented by constant combat but stumbled on.

There were, however, some Tlaxcalans who brought food and water to the Spanish camp. One day, about 50 Tlaxcalans came to the soldiers' camp. They gave Cortés a large amount of bread, cherries, and turkeys. They followed the soldiers around, asking them how they were doing and what their plans were. Suspiciously, they wandered about the camp, observing the guns and horses. One of Cortés's men warned the commander that these natives might be spies sent to find the army's weaknesses.

Cortés ordered his men to bring him one of the Tlaxcalans. He questioned the native through

Aguilar, and within an hour he confessed that he was a spy. He told Cortés that the spies had come to discover where the army could be easily attacked. He also said that the warriors planned to attack at night since the Tlaxcalans had had no luck defeating the Spanish during the day.

After the spy confessed, Cortés had several other Tlaxcalans brought to him. These natives also confessed to being spies and repeated the same story almost word for word. Cortés had all 50 Tlaxcalans seized and their hands cut off. He sent them back to their army and threatened to do the same to any other spies.

The freezing winds that swept through the passes kept the men awake at night. The rocky terrain made them footsore and fatigued. The soldiers became downhearted. They complained to Cortés that there was no way to win against these odds. Even the great war heroes Caesar and Alexander would not be foolish enough to risk continuing. Cortés himself was suffering from fever and an upset stomach. (Appropriately, he was the first victim of a sickness present-day tourists call Moctezuma's Revenge.) The soldiers asked him to turn back to

Villa Rica so they could build a ship and return to Cuba while they still had the chance. Of course, they reminded Cortés that the scuttled ships would have come in handy at this point.

Cortés answered their complaints with the firmness of a born leader. He scolded them by stating that they spoke rather boldly for men who were offering unsolicited advice. "As for observation, gentlemen," he continued, "that the most famous Roman captains never performed deeds equal to ours, you are quite right. If God helps us, far more will be said in future history books about our exploits than has ever been said about those in the past."[13]

Relief was closer than the listeners suspected. The Tlaxcalans too had become tired of battle. The majority of the chiefs were ready to make peace with their fair-skinned enemies. Xicotenga was the only chief who wanted to continue the war, but he was overruled. Finally, the natives made peace with the Spaniards, and Cortés's army spent several weeks in the city of Tlaxcala. The Tlaxcalans were glad to have a powerful ally against the Aztecs. They finally saw a great opportunity to crush their most despised enemy.

MOCTEZUMA WELCOMES CORTÉS

Moctezuma was not blind to the events taking place in his kingdom. Cortés had managed to conquer several cities along the way to Tenochtitlán. Oddly, Moctezuma reacted as if he was timid and scared. Even a less powerful chief like Xicotenga had waged war against the newcomers and made them fight for their very lives.

Tenochtitlán

In 1518, Tenochtitlán was the glittering, thriving capital of the Aztec Empire. The city was strategically located on an island, surrounded by water. The Aztecs built roads, or causeways, of high land across the lake to various other cities. There were three main causeways that led directly to the capital.

When Cortés and his men walked into the capital, they were amazed by its beauty, order, and cleanliness. Anywhere from 150,000 to 300,000 people lived in Tenochtitlán, making it one of the biggest cities in the world at the time. A web of canals also ran through the city. Natives paddled their way through the city on these "water streets."

Perhaps, Moctezuma was playing a waiting game. The Spanish had shown themselves to be unstoppable in war. Moctezuma may have been looking for their weak spot. He could make it a battle of wits, which Moctezuma no doubt thought he would win. The farther he lured the Spanish into his empire, the more vulnerable they would be. They were slowly moving toward the center of his

The buildings in Tenochtitlán were impressive. Cortés was especially amazed by the Great Temple. It was a mammoth structure, so magnificent, Cortés wrote, that "no human tongue could describe it." The wall that surrounded the temple was wide enough to hold a town of 500 people. At least 40 towers lined the walls. Some were so high that a staircase of 50 steps led up to only the main level.

Tenochtitlán was not built by crude, uncivilized people. The Aztecs were advanced in technology. They were much different from any natives the Spaniards had ever met. In many ways, they were more powerful than their conquerors.

This Mexican painting shows the Aztec city of Tenochtitlán, which once stood on the site of present-day Mexico City. The Aztecs built causeways across the lake to connect Tenochtitlán with other cities.

web. A part of him probably thought that the strangers had come for gold, silver, and precious stones, and not to conquer the country. If he gave them riches, they might leave. Or they might just be explorers of the region, in which case Moctezuma would be foolish not to make peace.

Cortés, however, thought he was weak and cowardly. He was not doing anything to help his people feel confident and hopeful. Around Tenochtitlán, people walked in terror and sorrow. One of Cortés's men wrote, "Fathers cried, 'Oh, my little ones, what will become of you?' Mothers cried, 'Little ones, how can you bear the horror that is coming to you?'"[14]

With an army of 4,000 natives, Cortés continued on to the capital city. As they neared the town, four Aztec chiefs came out to meet him. They brought rich gifts of gold and precious stones from Moctezuma. The chiefs begged Cortés to turn back and leave the city alone. The plea fell on deaf ears. Cortés had not crossed the Atlantic Ocean and the Caribbean, nor suffered freezing cold, war, and other hardships, to be bought off by a lesser prize.

On November 8, 1519, the epic journey came to a climax with a meeting between Moctezuma and Cortés. Multitudes of men, women, and children crowded the streets of Tenochtitlán. The strangers looked like creatures from another planet, but

As scores of people crowded the streets of Tenochtitlán, Cortés and Moctezuma met on November 8, 1519. This picture of friendship would not last long.

many Aztecs believed that they were gods sent to conquer them as had been the prophecy of Aztec religion. Moctezuma approached Cortés in a lavish litter, decorated with a canopy of green feathers, gold markings, and dangling silver, pearl, and turquoise pieces.

The marvelous sight amazed Cortés. He dismounted his horse, and the 50-year-old Aztec emperor descended from his litter. The two men bowed deeply to each other. Moctezuma welcomed Cortés and his men. Cortés pulled out a necklace made of colored glass beads on a gold chain that had been dipped in musk to give it a pleasant odor. He hung it around the emperor's neck and tried to embrace him. But the princes who stood around Moctezuma grabbed Cortés's arm and stopped him. This act was considered insulting to the Aztecs.

"Is it you?" Cortés asked. "Is it really you? Are you truly Moctezuma?"

"I am he," Moctezuma answered. He bowed again to Cortés. "Lord, you have reached your destination," he continued. "You are tired and weary. You have arrived in your city of Tenochtitlán. You have arrived to take possession of your throne. . . . Rest now. Welcome to your kingdom, lords!"

Cortés listened to the words being interpreted in front of him. He was pleased to hear of the emperor's graciousness, but knew it couldn't be trusted. But Cortés answered him gently, "Be glad, Moctezuma. Fear nothing. We love you greatly." [15] However, this facade of friendship was not destined to last.

Test Your Knowledge

1 How did Cortés deal with the four leaders of the rebellion against him?

    a. He sent them back to Cuba in irons.

    b. He marooned them on a deserted island.

    c. He set them adrift at sea in a small rowboat.

    d. He ordered two hanged, one flogged, and one to have his feet cut off.

2 Why did Cortés sink his own ships?

    a. He feared them falling into the hands of the Portuguese.

    b. He needed the wood to build a fortress.

    c. He hoped to prevent desertion.

    d. None of the above.

3 How did Cortés deal with the Tlaxcalan spies in his midst?

    a. He gave them over to the Aztecs.

    b. He had them drawn and quartered.

    c. He had their hands cut off.

    d. He had them beheaded.

4 What finally ended the Tlaxcalans' attacks on
the Spaniards?

   a. The natives had become battle weary and
     decided to trust Cortés.

   b. Cortés had the native chiefs killed.

   c. The Aztecs defeated the Tlaxcalans.

   d. None of the above.

5 How were Cortés and his army first received by
Moctezuma?

   a. With a raging battle

   b. With courtesy and grace

   c. With spies and plots of assassination

   d. None of the above

ANSWERS: 1. d; 2. c; 3. c; 4. c; 5. b

The Kidnap of Moctezuma

For six days, the mood at Tenochtitlán was peaceful. Moctezuma's men escorted the Spanish throughout the city. The soldiers marveled at the richly adorned royal palaces, decorated zoos, and exotic gardens. The temples sparkled with gold, silver, and bright green turquoise. The market squares bounced with chatter, as the townspeople bartered with Aztec merchants. The Aztecs rowed Cortés and his men around the glistening spiderweb of canals that weaved around the city.

Most of the soldiers had never seen a real city before. Compared with Tenochtitlán, Santo Domingo and Santiago were like shantytowns. Even Cortés had never visited a city of this grandeur. The gold, silver, and glittering stones no doubt sparked his greed. To capture a city of such treasure would be the greatest feat any explorer had ever achieved.

Although Moctezuma treated the Spaniards like his royal guests, they could feel the chill of treachery on the backs of their necks. They were in a delicate position—trapped inside the walls of a desperate city. They were able to defeat the Tlaxcalans on an open plain where they had room to maneuver. But how could they fight the Aztecs in the middle of a crowded city?

Cortés knew that to wait for the Aztecs' move would be foolish. His soldiers must strike the first blow—that was the Spanish way. Over the past days, the Spaniards noticed how much Moctezuma's subjects adored him. In this city, Moctezuma was the key to authority and order.

Cortés's advisor, Gonzalo de Sandoval, told him that they must kidnap the emperor and hold him hostage. Cortés was unsure whether kidnapping was the right action. He spent long hours pacing back and forth, contemplating this crucial move. In the past, he had always started mildly before releasing his brutal force. He feared a drastic action would drive the Aztecs to extreme hostility. Cortés decided that such a dangerous risk could not be taken.

But overnight, something changed his mind. Two Tlaxcalan messengers brought news that some Totonacs had attacked the Spanish town of Villa Rica, by order of the Aztecs. They killed seven Spaniards. The Aztecs had captured Cortés's town of refuge. Cortés realized the Aztecs now had the soldiers trapped. If he could not defeat Moctezuma, his men would have nowhere to go.

Cortés marched an army of 30 men across the town square to Moctezuma's palace. In firm but courteous words, Cortés told the emperor that he was under arrest for the murders at Villa Rica.

Moctezuma immediately sent officers to the coast to arrest the men responsible for the attack, but Cortés wasn't satisfied. He insisted that the emperor come with him.

The Spanish captains grew impatient. "What's the use of talking?" Juan Velázquez argued. "Either we take him or knife him. If we don't, we are dead men." [16]

Cortés was reluctant to use violent force. He wanted to uphold a good reputation as a conquistador. Men who were brutal to barbaric emperors in the New World might also be tempted to lay violent hands on civilized emperors in the Old World. Cortés did not want to be branded as a cruel and evil explorer who couldn't be trusted.

One of Cortés's interpreters, a woman named La Malinche, stepped in. She begged Moctezuma to go with the Spaniards. "I know they will treat you honorably," she said. "But if you stay here, you will die." [17]

So Moctezuma agreed to go calmly with the soldiers. Cortés took him to the palace of Axayácatl, where the Spanish soldiers were staying. He placed the emperor under heavy guard. The arrest of

Xaltelolco.

A seated Hernándo Cortés meeting with Aztec emissaries. Next to Cortés is La Malinche, his interpreter and companion. Today, many people see La Malinche as a heroine for the natives and the Spanish.

Moctezuma brought a deeper chill to the air, and the hearts of the soldiers pounded wildly at the thought of what would come.

MOCTEZUMA BECOMES A VASSAL

Cortés tried to make the emperor's imprisonment as tolerable as possible. Two to three weeks later, the

Aztecs involved in the attack on Villa Rica arrived. They admitted to starting the attack on the Spanish town. Cortés intended to prove that the Aztec thugs would not intimidate the Spaniards. He arrested all 15 men, tried them for murder, and sentenced them to death. To heighten the drama, Cortés ordered Moctezuma's hands and ankles bound in chains. He then had the 15 offenders burned to death.

Cortés meant for the sentencing to be an example of Spanish justice and to strike fear and obedience in the hearts of the Aztecs. But his plan backfired. For the natives, the victims were patriots and heroes. The violent method of execution made the Spaniards no less barbaric than the Aztecs. In addition, he committed an unforgivable act by putting Moctezuma in irons.

As if realizing his mistake, Cortés removed Moctezuma's fetters the same day. From that time forward, the emperor was shown complete respect. Although he could not freely move about the city, Moctezuma led his normal life.

Cortés took the role of Moctezuma's prime minister. He was especially glad to see the emperor become very fond of the Spanish servant whom

(continued on page 86)

La Malinche, Traitor or Heroine?

Some natives of Mexico scowl at the thought of La Malinche, called Doña Marina by the Spaniards. Natives name her a traitor and a harlot for her role in aiding Cortés as he conquered the Aztecs.

Marina was the daughter of a noble Aztec family. After the death of her father, a chief, her mother remarried and gave birth to a son. Marina's mother decided her new son should be the new ruler. One day, she gave Marina to some passing traders and proclaimed her dead from that moment on.

Eventually, Marina became a slave of the cacique of Tabasco. By the time Cortés arrived in Mexico, she had learned the Mayan dialects used in the Yucatán and still understood the Aztec language. The cacique offered Marina to Cortés as a slave, along with 19 other women. Cortés immediately noticed her command of the native languages and showed her special attention. He took her as his personal attendant.

Although some natives call her a traitor, Marina saved thousands of lives by helping

Cortés negotiate rather than slaughter. She served as an interpreter with the Cempoalans, the Tlaxcalans, and Moctezuma. Without her, Cortés may have failed in his conquest. In order to wage a successful campaign against the Aztecs, he needed to communicate with the other native groups. Marina made this possible.

During the conquest, Cortés and Marina fell in love. Throughout the campaign, the two remained loyal to each other. The couple even had a son, Don Martin Cortés. But Cortés knew his marriage with Catalina would make it impossible for him and Marina to be together. After the conquest, Cortés arranged a marriage between Marina and a respected Spanish knight named Don Juan Xamarillo.

Today, most people view Marina as a heroine of both the Mayans and the Spaniards. She was a remarkable interpreter, whom Cortés trusted as his "right-hand man," or rather "right-hand woman."

(continued from page 83)

Cortés assigned to him. Moctezuma and the Spanish captains also were on the friendliest terms. Cortés had the carpenters build sloops, or sailing ships. On some days, the emperor was escorted to the lake's edge and sat under a painted awning. He watched the Spanish mariners zig-zag their ships from one shore to the other. He laughed with delight when the gunners fired salutes in his honor.

As always, Cortés was thinking ahead. And the sloops were a genius decision. They would be powerful weapons in future warfare. They could be used to attack lakeside cities or carry troops from shore to shore. In case of a sudden emergency, the soldiers could make a quick escape to another landing.

Of course, gold was the first thought in all of Cortés's endeavors. He never stopped searching for it, and his main purpose was to find a way to get his hands on it. A Spanish carpenter discovered a chest of treasure hidden in a wall of the palace of Axayácatl. The Spaniards stared wide-eyed at the incredible wealth of gold, silver, and precious stones inside the box.

Cortés, however, immediately ordered his men to seal the chest and return it. He did not want to steal his riches. He wanted all spoils to belong to him legally. He asked Moctezuma to make a formal act of submission to Emperor Charles. To do this, Moctezuma had to summon his chiefs and rulers from every corner of the kingdom and get their approval.

Some chiefs refused to come to the capital. They openly stated their hostility to the Spaniards. And the ones who obeyed the call did not immediately consent either. Eventually, Moctezuma persuaded most of them to swear loyalty to the Roman emperor.

Meanwhile, more treasure had been found hidden in the walls of the palace. After Moctezuma swore loyalty to Charles, Cortés instructed him to send a tribute to the Roman emperor from the Aztec cities. Moctezuma led Cortés to a sealed room in the palace. He offered all the contents of the room as his tribute.

"Take this tribute which I have collected," Moctezuma said. "Only haste prevents there being more." He added, "Include in your letter to the emperor: This is sent to you by your loyal vassal Moctezuma." [18]

It took the Spaniards three days to take out the gold objects from the room. They sorted the pieces into three large heaps. The treasure was worth 600,000 pesos, or about $53,500, a huge amount of money at the time. The beautiful pieces of jewelry were spared, but the rest was broken up and melted down into gold bars.

At this point, trouble started. Cortés, the poor Medellín boy, stood before the stack of shining gold. He ordered that an amount of treasure equal to what would be sent to the emperor be saved for himself. This act was not necessarily unreasonable or greedy. After all, Cortés had sunk every bit of his money into the expedition. He also set aside an amount to repay Diego de Velázquez for his sunken fleet.

The next shares went to the captains, horsemen, musketeers, crossbowmen, and even the priests. There was little left over for the foot soldiers. The infantrymen were so insulted by their cut that they refused to take the small amount Cortés offered. Quarrels broke out in the ranks. Men had fistfights over card and dice games. Two men even drew swords and wounded each other. These squabbles weakened the morale and unity of the army.

CORTÉS FIGHTS THE GODS

It was not enough that Moctezuma had to swear loyalty to a Christian king. Cortés also wanted him to accept the Christian god. Even more so, he wanted Moctezuma to give up the hideous practice of human sacrifice. During their stay, the Spaniards had watched the number of victims climb. Cortés was not powerful enough to ban the Aztec religion and cause a revolt. But Cortés eventually lost his temper and put the expedition's success at terrible risk.

One day, Cortés and eight Spaniards took a walk in Tenochtitlán. They visited a shrine at the Great Temple. Stone images of idols covered the inside walls of the temple. Human blood pooled in the idols' mouths. Cortés stared at the wall and sadly sighed, "O God, why do you allow the Devil to be so much honored in this land?"

By this time, Aztec priests and townspeople had gathered there. Cortés turned to the people and said, "Here where you have these idols, there shall be the image of God and of his blessed mother. Bring me water to wash these walls, and we can remove all this stuff from here."

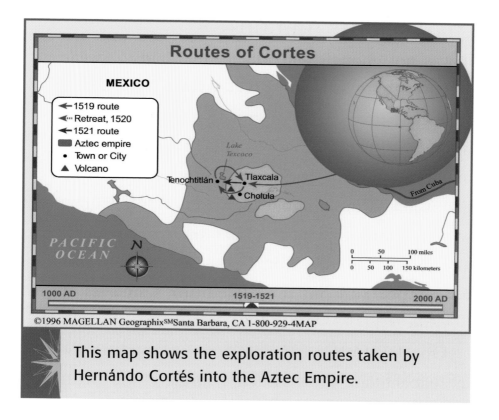

This map shows the exploration routes taken by Hernándo Cortés into the Aztec Empire.

The people laughed. "The whole land, as one, hold these as their gods," they replied. "All this is here by the power of Huitzilopochtli, whose creature we are. Everyone holds his parents and children as nothing compared to this god, and would . . . die for their gods."

Cortés turned to one of his men. "Go, call together 30 or 40 soldiers." He then shouted to the priests, "I shall be happy to fight for my God against your gods, who are nothing." He picked up an iron bar and leaped into the air, smashing the face of Huitzilopochtli between the eyes.[19]

In one minute, Cortés could have threatened his entire voyage. He went on to overturn the idols and roll them down the temple stairs. He ordered the temple washed clean of blood and set up statues of the Virgin Mary and other saints.

Anger boiled in Moctezuma and his people, but they did not show it. They believed that if the gods became angry, they would punish the Aztec people. But Cortés went on to destroy the idols in every chapel and wash the walls clean. He also forbade any more human sacrifices.

Suppressing the Aztec religion was sure to cause havoc. But Cortés was suddenly struck with another problem, one that had been brewing since the day he left Cuba. Diego de Velázquez was about to get his revenge.

Test Your Knowledge

1 What impressed Cortés and his men about the city of Tenochtitlán?

 a. Its size

 b. Its gold and jewels

 c. Its palaces and gardens

 d. All of the above

2 How did Cortés decide to defeat the Aztecs?

 a. On the open field of battle

 b. By sneak attack near Villa Rica

 c. By kidnapping Moctezuma

 d. None of the above

3 How did Cortés punish the Aztecs who had raided Villa Rica?

 a. He ordered them burned to death.

 b. He ordered them hanged.

 c. He ordered them thrown to the sharks.

 d. None of the above.

4 How would the treasure that Moctezuma gave as a tribute be valued today?

 a. About $1 million

 b. Slightly over $50,000

 c. Slightly less than $50,000

 d. About $10,000

5 Why did Cortés destroy all the idols in
   the temple?
   a. He wanted to end the practice of
      human sacrifice.
   b. He wanted the Aztecs to convert to
      Christianity.
   c. He had become enraged.
   d. All of the above.

ANSWERS: 1.d; 2. c; 3. a; 4. b; 5. d

Aztec
Uprising

Diego de Velázquez assembled a fleet of 19 ships,
1,400 men (900 of them Spanish), 80 horses, and
23 cannons. He chose Pánfilo de Narváez, who was from
Cortés's home province in Spain, to command the fleet.
Like Velázquez, Narváez had a personal score to settle
with Cortés. The fleet set sail in early March. It crossed

quickly and anchored at Villa Rica, where Cortés had made his own landing almost a year before.

Narváez's force was in every way stronger than Cortés's. Narváez thought his troops would easily defeat the rebel explorer. But Cortés had no doubt he would be able to deal with Narváez. He had reached Tenochtitlán with only a handful of men through using his wits. His troops fought their way through rough terrain and natives. They were veterans of this Mexican war—fearless and hardened by battle. More important, they were in possession of the land, and a large piece of the country's wealth was in their hands. They had much invested in this expedition and more to lose than Narváez's men.

After the attack on Villa Rica, Cortés sent the trusted Gonzalo de Sandoval and 70 men to the coast to re-establish order and control. It was Sandoval who received the first three messengers from Narváez. He immediately seized the officers, tied them in hammocks, and sent them off to Cortés in Tenochtitlán.

From the beginning, Cortés must have known that Velázquez would eventually send an army after him. But the arrival of Narváez was untimely. Cortés had made the mistake of dividing his army. Aside from the 70 men in Villa Rica, he had sent Juan Velázquez and 100 men in search of a deep seaport. At the time, they were 150 miles down coast.

But Cortés acted quickly. He sent messengers to Juan instructing him to meet the rest of the army near Villa Rica. Then, he divided the rest of his company into two units. Captain Pedro de Alvarado and 200 men would stay and guard Tenochtitlán. Cortés took the other 100 men on the march back to Villa Rica. The army left on May 4, 1520.

Along the way, Cortés sent letters of peace to Narváez. He believed it was wrong to battle against his own countrymen. Through bribery, he hoped to avoid a wasteful use of arms. Unfortunately, Narváez refused to bargain.

While Cortés was planning a strategy, Narváez was wasting time. He had too much confidence in his men. Instead of getting his troops ready, he spent his energies on plundering Totonac villages. Narváez's only plan was to barricade himself in the town of Cempoala and fight off Cortés's men—who he heard were approaching.

Actually, Cortés was only four miles away. He stood in the pouring rain, drilling his men with the

Diego de Velázquez, the governor of Cuba, sent Pánfilo de Narváez, above, to try to take down Cortés. In every way, Narváez's force was stronger than Cortés's.

details of that night's attack. Sandoval would lead the first strike with an army of about 80 men.

Rain spilling from the rim of his hat, Cortés instructed Sandoval to attack and take out Narváez's cannons. Cortés said he would follow with the rest of the army and lead a full-scale attack.

In the dead of night, Cortés launched his raid on Cempoala. Sandoval overran the guns in a single charge. His army drove most of Narváez's sleepy soldiers back to the center of town. They fled up the temple steps for safety. The heavy rains caused the horsemen to panic, and they retreated into the blackness.

By the time Cortés and his men arrived, Narváez was ready to surrender. The easy defeat that Narváez had expected had gone horribly wrong. The proud commander lost an eye in the brief but brutal skirmish. Cortés bribed Narváez's men into accompanying his troops back to Tenochtitlán. These additions boosted his army to 1,300 Spanish foot soldiers, 96 horsemen, 80 musketeers, and 80 crossbowmen. He also enlisted 2,000 Tlaxcalan warriors.

Cortés expected to rest his soldiers before returning to Tenochtitlán. But messengers from the Aztec capital brought some shocking news. The Aztecs had finally launched a rebellion.

THE DEATH OF MOCTEZUMA

According to the messengers, the Spanish soldiers were penned up in the palace. Their food and ammunition were running low. As soon as the messengers had finished telling their story, four Aztec caciques showed up.

They complained that they were innocently celebrating the feast day of Huitzilopochtli, when the Spaniards sprung on them with their swords, and set out to slaughter them one by one.

Apparently, Aztec representatives had asked Alvarado if they could observe their feast day. They assured the Spanish captain that it would be a strictly religious ceremony. Alvarado granted their request. A thick crowd gathered in the main city square, dancing and singing to the sounds of flutes and drums. At the end of the day, the Spaniards secretly shut off three gateways leading out of the square. Suddenly, a mass of soldiers charged through the remaining gate, slashing about in a cold fury. They spared no one, killing men, women, and children alike. Before long, puddles of blood filled the streets. Arms, legs, and heads littered the city square. The event later became known as the massacre of the Great Temple.

Alvarado claimed that as the day passed, the dancing became more intense and frantic. He worried that the Aztecs were getting ready to revolt. More likely, he saw the fancy clothes they wore—gold jewelry and headpieces. Alvarado was known as a greedy man. He probably murdered them to steal their riches.

On the way back to Tenochtitlán, Cortés and his men passed through one empty town after another. He had promised his men a triumphant march through the towns. But the only creatures to welcome them were a few stray turkeys and chickens. When they entered the capital, the same eerie silence hung heavy in the air. It was as if they had entered a dead and abandoned city.

Cortés marched straight to the palace of Axayácatl to deal with Alvarado. Whatever the reason for the attack, Alvarado had destroyed any hope for peace at Tenochtitlán. No amount of smooth talk could reverse the feelings of hatred alive in the city. Cortés was disgusted at the circumstances.

When Alvarado tried to explain himself, Cortés wouldn't let him finish.

"It was a bad thing and a big mistake," he barked. "I wish to God I had never heard of this business."[20]

For the first time, Cortés felt discouraged. His own captain had betrayed him. He undoubtedly thought, must I do everything myself? It seemed as if he must make all the decisions, unable to trust his closest officers.

The next day, June 25, Cortés sent out 400 men to patrol the quiet streets. Suddenly, an explosive roar broke the silence, and the Aztecs charged out of their houses in a furious attack. Taken completely by surprise, the soldiers ran back to the palace in utter confusion. A blanket of arrows and sling stones darkened the sky above the palace. The Spaniards rushed to defend the walls. But the Aztecs were already setting fire to the building. They were only pushed back when Cortés opened fire on them with muskets and cannons.

Hatred and revenge weren't the only reasons the Aztecs rebelled. They had a new leader. The Aztecs had tired of Moctezuma's passive attitude toward the Spaniards. He almost seemed more loyal to them than to his own people. Moctezuma's brother, Cuitláhuac, replaced him as emperor. Cuitláhuac had roused the people to war. The once-timid Aztecs were transformed into fierce warriors with unbreakable spirit and vigor. The Aztecs declared that they would wipe out every single Spaniard, even if 20,000 Aztecs had to die for each soldier killed. On the first day of battle, the Aztecs killed 10 soldiers and wounded 80.

The next day, the fighting was just as severe. Another 10 Spanish soldiers were killed, and another 80 wounded. Cortés began to realize that he must get his men out of the city to safety. He ordered the carpenters to build three wooden towers on wheels. They would be large enough to fit 20 cross-bowmen and musketeers. The shooters could fire their weapons from slits in the sides while foot soldiers and horsemen marched on either side of the tower. Cortés's plan was to escape through one of the main gateways with as few losses as possible.

Cortés's plan fell to pieces. The bridges outside the city had been burned and the drawbridges over the canals destroyed. Work on the towers ended. And Spanish casualties continued to climb.

In desperation, Cortés tried one last attempt at negotiations. Perhaps, if he had Moctezuma speak to the people, they would make peace. He took Moctezuma out on the palace balcony. They both hid behind shields for protection. The former emperor addressed his once-faithful subjects. Something he said provoked them to cry out in anger. An eruption of spears, arrows, and sling stones shot up at the two leaders. Moctezuma was hit and crumpled to the balcony floor.

The Spaniards carried the wounded ruler back to his apartment. He died three days later. Two Aztec prisoners carried Moctezuma's body out to be buried. The warriors claimed they did not know it was Moctezuma on the balcony. They could not see his face behind the shields and thought it was a trick. The Aztecs wept bitterly as they carried their dead king away.

CORTÉS'S RETREAT

Cortés released some prisoners to send to the Aztec leaders with a deal. If the Spanish could leave the city within eight days, they agreed to leave all the gold and treasure behind. This bargain

As the Aztecs rebelled against the Spanish, Cortés asked a captured Moctezuma to speak to the people in an effort to make peace. Moctezuma said something to provoke the people, and he was killed in a flurry of arrows and sling stones being shot at him.

was a trick. Cortés planned to leave Tenochtitlán immediately, in the middle of the night. His pitch-black attack had worked on Narváez. Hopefully, it would work again.

Because the bridges and drawbridges had been destroyed, Cortés had his carpenters hammer together a portable bridge. He created four columns of troops. The troops transported the cannons, the hostages, and the all-important treasure for the king. But much of the treasure had to be left behind. Cortés had the boxes of gold bars and jewels stacked in a hallway of the palace.

"I can do no more with these riches," he said. "There are 700,000 pesos worth. I shall give it over to any soldiers who care to take it. Otherwise we shall lose it to those dogs."[21] The soldiers weighed themselves down as heavily as they could.

Just before midnight on July 1, the soldiers quietly opened the doors of the palace. Trying to keep the strictest silence, the huge column of Spaniards crept through the city. A light rain fell on the darkened city. All seemed to be going well.

Suddenly, a shrill whistle blew in the darkness. Tens of thousands of Aztecs flooded the streets.

They had been waiting to ambush them. Confusion let loose among the column, which narrowed into a crooked snake. The soldiers had no choice but to push on. Canoes full of Aztecs landed on the beach and tore down the portable bridge.

Soldiers fell dead at every step. The hostages, including Moctezuma's sons and daughters, were killed in the madness. Others struggled back to the palace of Axayácatl, where they would eventually be captured and sacrificed at the Great Temple.

Some of the soldiers, including Cortés, managed to escape across a canal to the plaza at Tlacopán. Alvarado made it over with an amazing jump of his horse from one side to the other. The survivors watched the slaughter from the other side of the shore. When they saw that no other soldiers were coming through the gateways, they burst into tears. Cortés stood beneath a huge cypress tree, weeping like a father who had lost his children. This event of Cortés's conquest became known as *La Noche Triste*, or the Night of Sorrow.

But the battle was far from over. The Aztecs kept Cortés and the other survivors penned in the plaza for the whole next day. More than 150 Spaniards,

2,000 natives, and 50 horses were added to the dead. Cortés later wrote, "No horse could run, no horseman lift his arms, no infantryman place one foot in front of the other."[22] That night, the soldiers left their campfires burning in the plaza to mislead the enemy. Because of their smaller numbers, they made a more successful escape. The enemy did not notice them disappear until dawn. Again, the Aztecs went after the Spaniards. By nightfall, Cortés had only traveled seven or eight miles.

During the night, a Tlaxcalan chief came into Cortés's camp. He told the commander that he could safely lead the soldiers to Tlaxcala. Cortés had to trust him. Any other choice would certainly lead his men to death. The soldiers staggered wounded and weary to the town of Otumba. After three days of marching, they had only covered 40 miles.

The next morning, July 7, they hobbled out of Otumba and continued their trek. They had gone no more than three miles, when the men raised their faces to a terrifying sight. A line of what looked like the entire Aztec army rose up against the rocky skyline. They were surrounded. This time, escape seemed impossible.

(continued on page 110)

Ancient Mexico

Before the rise of the Aztecs, at least three great civilizations ruled in Mexico: the Olmecs, the Mayas, and the Toltecs. Ancient Mexico and Central America are historically known as Mesoamerica. This term refers to both the geographical area and the cultural traditions of its early peoples. The Olmecs were dominant from about 1200 B.C. to about 400 B.C. They developed hierarchical city-state kingdom that subsequent Mexican civilizations used. The Olmecs lived in the lowlands of south-central Mexico, roughly where the Veracruz and Tabasco regions are today.

The Maya civilization flourished in Southern Mexico and Central America from A.D. 250 to 900. Mayas built huge religious cities that included ball-game courts and homes. They developed a method of hieroglyphic language. In this form of writing, a picture or symbol represents a word, syllable, or sound. Mayas also created an elaborate and complex calendar system. This calendar was the most accurate system known to humans before the Gregorian calendar of the 1500s. The Gregorian calendar is the system most widely used today.

About 900, the Maya centers were mysteriously abandoned. Some Mayas migrated to the Yucatán

Peninsula. Until the arrival of the Spanish in the 1500s, the Maya civilization was centered in this region.

In the 900s, the Toltecs rose to power in central Mexico. They were the first people of the region to leave a relatively complete history. Tula was the Toltec capital. The ruins of this city are near the present-day town of Tula de Allende, about 50 miles north of Mexico City.

In the 1100s, a drought hit the north central region of Mexico. Desperate and starving people from the north wandered southward into Toltec territory. Eventually, these people overtook the Toltecs and forced them out of Tula. Toltec survivors moved south to the Valley of Mexico and joined other peoples.

The last nomadic peoples in the valley were the Mexica, more commonly known as the Aztec. Some archaeologists think that the Aztecs may have come from northwest Mexico. However, according to Aztec legend, they came from Aztlan around 1100. This mythical place was north of the Valley of Mexico. The Aztecs traveled to the valley, guided by the chirps of their sun and war god, Huitzilopochtli, which means "hummingbird on the left."

(continued from page 107)

Cortés's heart sunk. After a moment, he took a deep breath, and faced the enemy with the bravery of 100 men. Cortés took two heavy blows to his head from sling stones. Despite his wounds, he fought the Battle of Otumba with unbreakable resolve. He rode around the field, instructing and encouraging his men. The soldiers slashed their way through the Aztec army. Finally, the Aztecs retreated. The victory not only lifted the men's spirits, it proved to the Aztecs that the Spanish fire had not been put out.

Test Your Knowledge

1 Why did Narváez believe it would be easy to defeat Cortés?

   a. Narváez had more men than Cortés.

   b. Narváez had more weapons than Cortés.

   c. Narváez had an easily defensible location at Cempoala.

   d. All of the above.

2 How did Cortés defeat Narváez?

   a. Cortés bribed the local tribesmen to do his fighting for him.

   b. Cortés drilled his men, then attacked Narváez and his cannons at night.

   c. Cortés accepted Narváez's offer of peace before hostilities broke out.

   d. None of the above.

3 How did Alvarado betray Cortés?

   a. He stole Aztec gold while Cortés was away fighting Narváez.

   b. He restored Moctezuma to power without Cortés's permission.

   c. He launched a bloody massacre of the Aztecs during a feast day.

   d. None of the above.

4 What became of the wheeled battle towers Cortés
ordered built?

a. The plan worked and the towers helped the
Spaniards escape the city.

b. The plan worked, but the towers were burned
in the process.

c. The plan failed, as Cortés realized that key
bridges had been burned.

d. None of the above.

5 How did Moctezuma die?

a. He was killed by his own people while trying
to quiet the rebellion.

b. The Spaniards had him beheaded after he
failed to quiet the rebellion.

c. He caught smallpox.

d. He took his own life after losing power.

ANSWERS: 1. d; 2. b; 3. c; 4. c; 5. a

Conquest!

Finally, the Spaniards made it to Tlaxcala on July 12. They did not enter the city the all-conquering heroes as they had hoped to. But they had inflicted one major defeat on the enemy. Cortés was relieved that his Tlaxcalan allies were still willing to stand by him.

Of his army, only about 500 men remained. The few soldiers left were mostly Cortés's original men. It seemed as if Cortés was worse off than in the beginning, but he was more confident in his army than ever. The survivors of this expedition were the bravest and the best.

Cortés refused to march back to Villa Rica. He wanted to stay in the area and strike back as soon as possible. He recruited Tlaxcalan warriors and taught them the Spanish methods of warfare. In the end, 100,000 natives pledged their loyalty to Cortés; 20,000 of them were Tlaxcalans.

The harsh experiences of the past year and a half had changed Cortés. In battle, he suffered two head wounds and lost the use of two of his fingers. He had suffered alongside his men through freezing nights and sweltering days. He watched friends get struck down in battle. The 35-year-old commander looked haggard and stern. But he wasn't finished yet.

He sent an army force under the command of Cristóbal de Olid to attack the Aztec community of Tepeyac. This town was on the northern side of the lake at Tenochtitlán. Tepeyac was in command of the northern entrance to the capital—the most hidden of all sides. If the Spaniards took control of the city, they could conceal their final advance on Tenochtitlán. Also, Tepeyac had a rich countryside near Tlaxcalan territory. Furthermore, on the Night of Sorrows, the people of Tepeyac captured 16 Spaniards. They were either immediately killed or offered as sacrifices. Cortés had a score to settle. With the help of his Tlaxcalan warriors, Olid successfully conquered the city.

Meanwhile, Cortés was preparing a new weapon—a sailing fleet. The Aztecs had destroyed the ships he had built in Tenochtitlán, the ones Moctezuma enjoyed so much. Cortés replaced them with a squadron of 13 vessels. The ships were strong enough to carry cannons and large platoons of soldiers. Carpenters used timber from the local pine forests and the sails Cortés had stripped from the sunken fleet.

On December 28, 1520, Cortés led his army out of Tlaxcala. They marched in confident strides. In the hands of a capable leader, the soldiers were certain they could conquer anything in their path.

THE MOBILE WAR

The army reached the Aztec city of Texcoco on December 31. Because Texcoco and Tenochtitlán had strong ties, Cortés expected a hostile encounter. Instead, he found the town deserted. The ruler and chieftains had fled to Tenochtitlán. Cortés decided to occupy the city and made it his headquarters for the next four months.

Cortés's plan was not an immediate attack of Tenochtitlán. He planned to march along the shores of the lake and cut off access to supplies and allies. At the beginning of January, Cortés led a force of 250 Spanish soldiers and 2,000 natives to the town of Iztapalapa. Iztapalapa marked the southern entrance to the city. The city was gruesomely taken, with 6,000 men, women, and children killed.

After Iztapalapa, Cortés made his second move of the mobile war. He turned to Chalco. Sandoval led a quick raid and easily conquered the town. With these areas secured, Cortés took the expedition north and then down the west side all the way to Tlacopán (Tacuba). Along the way, the army stormed some of the lakeside towns, and others surrendered. Six months earlier, Cortés stood weeping under a tree in Tlacopán. This time, he shed no tears.

Cortés spent six days at Tlacopán observing the defenses of the capital. The Aztecs in the city were ready for a fight. They ran out on the causeways—high roads over the water—and provoked the Spanish soldiers. "Come on in, and have a good time!" they shouted. "Here you will die, as you did before."[23] The Spaniards tried to get them to surrender. "You will starve to death," they answered. "We have you trapped."

"We need no food, because we will eat both you and the Tlaxcalans," they replied.[24]

The Aztecs absorbed much of their energy from their young new ruler, Cuauhtémoc. Moctezuma's brother, Cuitláhuac, was emperor only a few months before he died from the European disease small-pox. The new emperor was fearless and anxious for battle.

Cortés tried to make peace with Tenochtitlán. But it was no use. The Aztecs refused to surrender. The commander continued invading towns around the capital. The Aztecs fought with spirit and fury but finally fell to the Spaniards.

On January 15, Cortés arrived at Xochimilco, a city on the lake. The army plunged into another series of battles. Wave after wave of enemy canoes landed on the beach. During one fight, Cortés's horse collapsed from exhaustion. An Aztec warrior immediately grabbed him by the arm. Luckily, a Tlaxcalan warrior and a young Spanish soldier jumped to his rescue. The soldier took three slashes with a sword defending his commander.

Cuauhtémoc tried his best to surround and overtake the Spaniards. But after three days of fighting, the Spanish-Tlaxcalan army defeated the Aztecs at Xochimilco. The soldiers suffered a blow to their morale, however. The fearlessness of the natives surprised them. The Aztecs fought as if they were going to win the war. Perhaps conquering Tenochtitlán would not come as easily as they had thought.

THE FALL OF TENOCHTITLÁN

Cortés led his ragged soldiers back to Texcoco. The men recuperated quickly. In early May, Cortés separated the army into three companies. He gave one to Sandoval, one to Alvarado, and one to Olid. Soon, up to half a million troops would engage in an epic war. The trophy was one of the largest cities in the world at that time.

Alvarado and Olid moved their companies out on May 10. They took the north route to the west bank of the lake. Sandoval later led the third division south to recapture Iztapalapa. Alvarado occupied Tlacopán, while Olid went on to Coyoacán. Both of these towns commanded the main causeway to the city. In war, the Aztecs destroyed anything of their own that might benefit the enemy. When the captains arrived at their posts, they found holes and barriers in the causeway. The Aztecs were preparing for a long siege, confident that the enemy would eventually tire and quit. Cortés ordered Olid to cut the great water aqueduct, cutting off Tenochtitlán's fresh water supply. By robbing the city of food and water, Cortés hoped to force the Aztecs to surrender.

The commander departed with his own company aboard the new fleet. On all sides, the entire war for the city depended on the water battles. Cortés later commented that the ships "held the key to the war." The city could not have been defeated by a land attack alone. The first fight set the standard for water battles, and the Spanish ships dominated the arena. The winds pushed the ships speeding across the water, crashing through the fragile Aztec canoes. Cannons and muskets blew the enemy craft to pieces. Many Aztecs jumped out of their boats only to drown in the lake.

On land, however, the battle was not as one-sided. Cortés wanted to pen up his enemy by blocking the city's five land exits. Day after day, soldiers and warriors crowded the causeways. They stumbled over stones, spears, and arrows. Any barricade the army overran during the day was lost at night. The soldiers fought all day to gain a few yards, only to lose them the next day.

It was a bloody and gruesome fight. Bodies floated in the water and lay unburied on the causeways. Finally, it appeared as if the Aztecs won. They broke through the line of infantrymen, who turned and ran.

"Stop, stop, gentlemen!" Cortés called. "Stand firm! What do you mean by turning your backs?"[25] But he couldn't stop them. Suddenly, an Aztec warrior speared Cortés in the leg, knocking him to the ground. The same young soldier who had saved

Cortés's soldiers battle the Aztecs for the city of Tenochtitlán. After three months of tireless and gruesome fighting, the Spanish-Tlaxcalan army captured the city in August 1521.

his life the first time again came to his rescue. This time, the boy died trying to protect him. Just in the nick of time, his soldiers pulled Cortés to safety. And the army retreated to Texcoco.

After a three-day lull, Cortés and his army came back and fought with renewed strength. They pushed the Aztec forces off the causeways and into the streets of Tenochtitlán. After three weeks of end-less combat, the soldiers had broken into the city.

Cortés finally decided that the only way to defeat the Aztecs was to destroy Tenochtitlán. He ordered a water and ground attack, and commanded his army not to advance until every building, wall, and roof had been leveled to the ground.

The soldiers destroyed the city inch by inch. Still, the Aztecs refused to give up. They ran from house

The Spanish Hand in Mexico

The Spanish conquest of the Aztec Empire gave way to a culture change throughout Mexico. Before long, the Spanish hand touched everything from language to art. Soon after Cortés took over, there was widespread intermarriage between the Spanish and the natives. By the 1600s, many natives had adopted the Spanish language. Today, as many as 100 native languages are still spoken in Mexico, but no one primary language next to Spanish prevails. The most important native language is Nahuatl, used by more than a million Mexicans. Maya is the next main language, which is spoken by 14 percent of natives.

to house, fighting to the bitter end. For a week, the soldiers fought in the city square. Images of the massacre stood everywhere they turned. The stench of unburied bodies hung in the air. It was a horrible and gruesome sight.

Finally, on August 13, 1521, after three months of tireless battle, Tenochtitlán fell to the Spanish-Tlaxcalan army. The war was over. Cuauhtémoc fled the city in a speedy canoe. But he was quickly

Mexican art is a blend of native traditions and Spanish influences. Before the Spaniards arrived, Aztecs had their own arts, such as ceramics, music, poetry, sculpture, and weaving. After the conquest, many natives converted to Roman Catholicism, the religion of the Spanish colonists. Native artists began mixing their intricate designs and bright colors with European techniques and religious themes. The result was a new unique Mexican style. For example, Mexican churches of this time period combine Spanish architecture with the decorative touches of the natives who built them.

An old church in the Sierra Madre mountains of Mexico. After the conquest, churches built around that time combined Spanish architecture with the decorative touches of the natives.

captured by one of Cortés's men and brought before the conqueror.

"I have assuredly done my duty in defense of my city and my vassals, and I can do no more,"

Cuauhtémoc sobbed. "Take that dagger that you have in your belt, and strike me dead immediately."[26]

Cortés answered him, "I admire you as a brave emperor. I only wish you would have surrendered when you knew you had lost. You could have saved many of your people's lives."[27] He then ordered his men to put Cuauhtémoc and his family under friendly guard. With the defeat of the Aztec Empire, Cortés could now call himself one of the world's greatest conquistadors.

That evening as peacefulness fell on Tenochtitlán, a rain began to pour. During the night, lightning flashed across the black sky, and thunder shook the earth. The storm brought an eerie end to months of death and ruin. The rain relentlessly pounded the earth as if cleansing itself from the puddles of spilled blood.

Test Your Knowledge

1 Even before the grueling battle at Tenochtitlán, Cortés had sustained several injuries, including

    a. the loss of his left foot and eye.

    b. a broken arm from a stone.

    c. two head injuries and loss of the use of two fingers.

    d. none of the above.

2 Why were ships so important to the Spaniards in their war against the Aztecs?

    a. Much of Tenochtitlán was surrounded by water.

    b. Cortés knew how to fight sea battles, but was inexperienced on land.

    c. The Aztecs had an excellent navy.

    d. None of the above.

3 In all, how long was the battle for control of Tenochtitlán?

    a. Three months

    b. Three weeks

    c. Three years

    d. Three days

4 What became of the young Spaniard who twice rushed to aid Cortés in battle?

    a. He was hailed as a hero and made an official conquistador.

    b. He received a large parcel of land as reward for his efforts.

    c. He was killed in battle while defending Cortés.

    d. None of the above.

5 What did Cortés do with Cuauhtémoc after the Spanish victory?

    a. Cortés had him beheaded.

    b. Cortés put him under friendly guard.

    c. Cortés allowed him to commit ritual suicide with a dagger.

    d. None of the above.

ANSWERS: 1. c; 2. a; 3. a; 4. c; 5. b

10

"I Am the Man!"

The end of the Aztec war brought about the beginning of Spanish America. Cortés's work was far from over. Ahead was the rebuilding of what is now Mexico City. Cortés had great plans for this city, which would be the grandest of all in the New World. But first, Tenochtitlán needed to be cleaned up. Soldiers leveled

After conquering Mexico, Hernándo Cortés took his place as ruler of the land. He began living like a king, with servants waiting on him everywhere he went.

any walls still standing. They cleared the rubble and carted the bodies away.

Cortés conquered Mexico, and he took his place as its rightful ruler. The treasures Cortés had sent to Spain impressed King Charles, who rewarded his service. Cortés became governor of New Spain and captain-general of its army. He began living like a king. He moved into a palace in Coyoacán, which was richly decorated and had a beautiful view. Servants waited on him wherever he went. Throughout the kingdom of New Spain, natives threw themselves to the ground whenever he walked past. His wealth and glory made some of his captains jealous. Before long, he had many enemies in his kingdom.

EXPLORING HONDURAS

The urge to conquer still ran strong in Cortés's veins. Near the end of 1523, Cortés sent expeditions to explore and conquer lands south of New Spain. Alvarado invaded the area that is today Guatemala and El Salvador. He easily defeated the natives there and set up a Spanish colony. Cortés assigned Olid to take over Honduras and rule it for him.

But Olid had other plans. Soon after arriving in Honduras, he betrayed Cortés. Honduras was a rich land, an important location in the pearl fisheries of the Pacific Coast of Central America. Olid wanted the riches for himself and wanted to be an independent ruler of the country.

When Cortés heard about Olid's rebellion, he was furious. Cortés never asked to be a beloved captain, only obeyed. After all they had been through on the conquest, Olid's betrayal was a serious blow to Cortés. He decided to make the expedition himself, find his treacherous captain, and punish him.

This decision was the biggest mistake of Cortés's life. He deserted his post as governor of a new country. The expedition left in October 1524. This army was nothing like the one he had first led through Mexico. Cortés traveled with every luxury of a prince. He brought cooks, butlers, dancers, musicians, and even jugglers. He also brought along Cuauhtémoc. He feared that the former emperor of Tenochtitlán might try to lead a revolt while he was away from the country.

At first, the journey went well. They had no troubles during the entire 350-mile trek east to Coatzacoalcos. Instead of traveling to Honduras by sea, the easy way, Cortés chose to march overland. The land route covered hundreds and hundreds of miles in some of the worst jungle on Earth. Cortés quickly realized it was a bad decision. The terrain was a maze of thick forests, mountain ranges, swampland, and winding rivers. Each step taken through the dark jungle had to be opened with hatchets and swords.

The march across Honduras turned out to be one of the greatest feats of endurance in human history. The soldiers faced hunger, thirst, flies, and mosquitoes. They had no idea where the next village was or how far they would have to travel to get there. More than once, they lost their way, fearing they would die before anyone could find them. Once, even the native scouts thought they were lost for

The Death of Cortés's Wife

In July 1522, Cortés got an unexpected visitor in New Spain. His wife, Catalina, arrived from Cuba. Inwardly, Hernándo was not pleased by her appearance. He had not invited her. Catalina never really loved Hernándo, but she felt entitled to some of his fortune. Despite his feelings, Hernándo held a great celebration in her honor.

One evening in August, Hernándo and Catalina had a violent argument at the dinner table. Catalina stormed off to her room. Later, Hernándo went to visit her and found her praying in silence. He noticed tears running down her cheeks.

"Why do you cry?" Hernándo asked.

"Let me alone. I feel like letting myself die," she replied.

good. Like always, Cortés confidently took charge. "Northwest," he ordered and pointed through the trees. The army ended up in the center square of the town they were trying to find.

The soldiers begged Cortés to turn around. But their pleas were met by his iron will. He refused to let the wilderness beat him. The army zig-zagged from one village to another, scrounging for food and supplies.

Hernándo put his arm around her. He called to her maids, who then undressed her for bed. A few hours later, the maids heard voices in Catalina's rooms. They swung open the doors.

"Bring some lights," Hernándo yelled. "I believe Doña Catalina is dead."* The maids brought in candles and saw the lovely woman lying lifeless in Hernándo's arms. Her necklace of golden beads was broken, and several dark spots colored her neck. Cortés went to his room. He locked his door and flew into a frenzy, banging his head against the wall and screaming in sorrow. Some people believed Cortés strangled his wife. No one knows the truth, but the suspicions floated above him like a black cloud.

* Madariaga, Salvador de, *Hernán Cortés: Conqueror of Mexico*, Garden City, NY: Doubleday, 1969, p. 417.

Finally, they came to a river that had flooded its banks. It was so enormous that even Cortés considered turning back to Mexico. But he vowed not to let his fear and despair defeat him. Despite the grumbling of his army, the men built a bridge with more than 1,000 beams. The smallest one was as thick as a man's body.

At this point, a native spy came running to Cortés. He warned that the Tenochtitlán emperor planned to kill Cortés and his captains and take back his throne. Cortés ordered Cuauhtémoc to be brought to him, and asked if he planned to rise against him. Cuauhtémoc admitted he had no love for the Spaniards, who destroyed his city and people, but he said only a fool would plan a rebellion in the middle of nowhere.

The treachery couldn't have come at a worse time. The hard expedition had already pushed Cortés's patience to the limit. He refused to believe the chief. He never trusted him from the beginning. He sentenced Cuauhtémoc to be hanged. Even Cortés's hardened veterans thought the act was cruel and unjust.

At a village in Tanina, Cortés finally received the news he had been waiting for. A native woman said she had seen Spaniards on the coast just two days earlier. These Spaniards could be Olid's men. Cortés sent Sandoval to find them. He brought back word of Olid's death.

Apparently, the conquistador Francisco de las Casas arrived with a fleet to overpower Olid. But a fierce storm dashed the ships against the coast and destroyed them. Olid captured Las Casas and another conquistador, Gil Dávila. He made them his prisoners, but they were free to come and go as they pleased. He even ate his meals with them.

One evening, Las Casas said jokingly, "Sir Captain, keep a sharp eye out. Someday, I may try to kill you."

Olid broke out in a hearty laugh and tipped his head back. Las Casas and Gil Dávila lunged at him and stabbed him in the throat. "For the King and for Cortés against this tyrant!" they shouted. They then hung him until he was dead.[28]

Unable to get his revenge on Olid, Cortés finally decided to return to New Spain. His absence had caused complete chaos. Cortés's enemies spread rumors that he was dead. They took over his castle and executed his cousin, whom Cortés had left in charge. He landed at last at Villa Rica on May 24, 1526, 19 months after his departure. On the 15-day trip back to Mexico City, natives in every town greeted Cortés with joyful cheers. They scattered flowers on the ground in front of him. Their love and devotion deeply moved Cortés. He immediately restored order, and threw his guilty enemies into prison.

News of the mayhem reached the royal court in Spain. Velázquez and his friends set out to make Cortés look like a traitor and a murderer. Charles V believed Velázquez's accusations and appointed Luis Ponce de León to take over as chief justice in New Spain. Cortés knew the only way to set things straight was to go to Spain and explain his actions to the king.

CORTÉS LOSES MEXICO

Cortés arrived in Spain in the spring of 1528. His country welcomed him with the gratitude he deserved. He was treated with every courtesy and hailed the conquering hero.

Certainly, Charles V appreciated Cortés's efforts. After all, the conqueror had brought great riches to the Spanish treasury. He treated Cortés like royalty, but refused to grant him the one thing he desired— to be reinstated governor of New Spain. Charles did, however, appoint Cortés captain-general of the army.

King Charles of Spain appreciated Cortés's efforts and treated him well. But he did not grant Cortés the one thing he wanted—to be reinstated as governor of New Spain.

Disappointed, Cortés returned to Mexico in 1530. Don Antonio de Mendoza took the coveted position of viceroy—or governor. Cortés and Mendoza argued bitterly about land boundaries and other issues. But Mendoza was a proud man and would not let the aging conqueror meddle in his government.

Cortés decided to try his hand at another expedition. In 1535, he set sail with three ships to find a water route connecting the Caribbean Sea to the Pacific Ocean. This expedition also turned disastrous. Two of the ships were wrecked in a storm, taking down with them much of the crew and supplies. After months of hunger, thirst, and wandering, the last beaten vessel carried the soldiers home.

Cortés got sick of the constant bickering with Mendoza. The viceroy never listened to Cortés anyway. In 1540, the fed-up conqueror sailed back to Spain with his two sons. The last seven years of his life were filled with disappointment and misery. His countrymen seemed to forget about the conqueror of the Aztecs. That was 20 years before, and younger men were now sending riches from the New World to Spain. Cortés wondered if the great explorer, too, had been conquered.

Finally, he decided to give up his search for glory and return home. He traveled to Seville, where he would rent a ship to take him to Villa Rica. The bustling city brought a flood of old memories back to Cortés. When he was 19, he set sail for the Indies from this very port. He recalled how young and ambitious he was. But that seemed so long ago.

While waiting for his ship, Cortés became sick with a high fever. He couldn't eat, and he was too weak to make the voyage home. He died on December 2, 1547, at the age of 62. His body was taken back to New Spain and buried in a church near the spot where he and Moctezuma first met.

While trudging across the Valley of Mexico, Cortés told his men that history books would say more about their conquest than any other. He was right. Sadly, the epic value of the conquistador wasn't recognized during his lifetime. One story paints a picture of Cortés's lost fame. One day, in the streets of Spain, Cortés saw the royal carriage approaching. He threw himself on it and called to the man inside. "Who is this man?" Charles V asked.

"I am the man," cried Cortés, "who brought to Your Majesty more kingdoms than your father left you towns!" But the coach pushed on, and Cortés was swallowed up by the crowds in the street.[29]

Test Your Knowledge

1 Which of the following best characterizes Cortés's trip through Honduras?
   a. A glorious trip across easy terrain
   b. A dismal trudge through jungles and swamps
   c. An easy river voyage on rafts
   d. None of the above

2 How did Cortés punish Olid for his betrayal?
   a. He had Olid stabbed and hanged.
   b. He had Olid beheaded.
   c. He had Olid burned at the stake.
   d. Olid was murdered before Cortés reached him.

3 Why, in the end, did Cortés order the death of Cuauhtémoc?
   a. He wanted to crush the Aztecs once and for all.
   b. He believed the former Aztec leader was plotting against him.
   c. Cortés was deranged with fever from malaria.
   d. None of the above.

4 Why did King Charles remove Cortés as governor of Mexico?
   a. The king had a grudge against Cortés.
   b. The king wanted his nephew to have the job.
   c. Cortés's old enemy Velázquez had planted rumors with the king.
   d. None of the above.

5 Which of the following best characterizes Cortés in the final years of his life?
   a. A respected country squire
   b. A hunted pirate
   c. A bitter, forgotten hero
   d. None of the above

ANSWERS: 1. b; 2. d; 3. b; 4. c; 5. c

1485   Hernándo Cortés is born in Medellín, Spain, to Martín Cortés de Monroy and Catalina Pizarro Altamirano.

1499   Hernándo goes to study grammar at his uncle's home in Salamanca.

1504   Cortés sails to the West Indies.

1518   Cortés signs an agreement with Diego de Velázquez, governor of Cuba, to lead an expedition to Mexico; the fleet sets sail from Santiago on November 18.

1519   Cortés's fleet finally sails from Cuba on February 10, landing at Cozumel several days later; the Spaniards

1485 Hernándo Cortés is born in Medellín, Spain

1499 Hernándo goes to study grammar at his uncle's home in Salamanca

1520 Aztecs revolt against the Spanish; Moctezuma is killed during a peace talk

1485

1504 Cortés sails to the West Indies

1518 Cortés agrees to lead an expedition from Cuba to Mexico

1522 Cortés's wife, Catalina, dies

1521 Cortés's army conquers Tenochtitlán

arrive at Cempoala on June 3; from September 2 to 20, the Spanish Army battles the Tlaxcalans; the Tlaxcalans end up as Cortés's allies; Cortés peacefully enters Tenochtitlán on November 8; on November 14, Cortés places Moctezuma II, the Aztec emperor, under arrest.

1520   Cortés learns that Velázquez has sent a fleet commanded by Pánfilo de Narváez to overthrow him; Cortés leaves Tenochtitlán for Villa Rica with an army of 100 soldiers on May 4; Cortés's men easily defeat Narváez; Cortés learns that Alvarado had led the Great Temple massacre; Cortés returns

1524 Cortés leads an expedition to Honduras

1526 Cortés loses his powers as governor

1540 The aging conqueror returns to Spain, where he is all but forgotten

1547

1535 Cortés leads an expedition to find a sea route from the Caribbean to the Pacific

1547 Cortés dies at the age of 62

to Tenochtitlán on June 24; Cuitláhuac becomes the new ruler of Tenochtitlán; Aztecs revolt against the Spanish; Moctezuma is killed during a peace talk; the Spaniards suffer terrible losses on June 30, the Night of Sorrows.; Cortés's army has a surprising victory over the Aztecs on July 7 in the Battle of Otumba.

1521   After Cuitláhuac dies from smallpox, young Cuauhtémoc becomes the new emperor of Tenochtitlán; Cortés's army of Spanish and Tlaxcalans attack Tenochtitlán in May; a bloody war follows; the army enters the city in June; in July, Cortés realizes the only way to defeat the Aztecs is to destroy the city; on August 13, soldiers capture Cuauhtémoc; the war for Tenochtitlán ends.

1522   Cortés's wife, Catalina, dies in his arms in August.

1524   Cortés leads an expedition to Honduras in October.

1526   Cortés returns to New Spain in May; his powers as governor are stripped from him by Charles V.

1528   In the spring, Cortés goes to Spain to explain himself to the emperor; he is re-appointed captain-general of the army, but is not awarded the governorship.

1530   Cortés returns to New Spain brokenhearted.

1535   Cortés leads a foolish expedition to find a sea route from the Caribbean to the Pacific.

1540 The aging conqueror returns to Spain, where he is all but forgotten.

1547 Hernándo Cortés dies on December 2, while waiting to take a ship back to New Spain, at the age of 62.

Chapter 1
Leave None Without a Wound

1. Jon Ewbank Manchip White, *Cortés and the Downfall of the Aztec Empire*, New York: St. Martin's Press, 1971, pp. 228–229.

Chapter 3
We Shall Conquer

2. Francisco Lopez de Gomara, *Cortés: The Life of the Conqueror by His Secretary*, Berkeley: University of California Press, 1964, p. 25.

3. Bernal Diaz del Castillo, *The Discovery and Conquest of Mexico, 1517–1521*, New York: Farrar, Straus, and Cudahy, 1956, p. 33.

Chapter 4
The Conquest Begins

4. Jon Ewbank Manchip White, *Cortés and the Downfall of the Aztec Empire*, New York: St. Martin's Press, 1971, p. 162.

5. Ibid., p. 168.

6. Ibid., p. 169.

7. Ibid., p. 172.

Chapter 5
Moctezuma

8. Ibid., p. 177.

9. Ibid., p. 178.

10. Ibid., p. 132.

Chapter 6
March to Tenochtitlán

11. Ibid., p. 184.

12. Ibid., p. 185.

13. Ibid., p. 191.

14. Ibid., p. 196.

15. Salvador de Madariaga, *Hernán Cortés: Conqueror of Mexico*, Garden City, NY: Doubleday, 1969, p. 240.

Chapter 7
The Kidnap of Moctezuma

16. Jon Ewbank Manchip White, *Cortés and the Downfall of the Aztec Empire*, New York: St. Martin's Press, 1971, p. 260.

17. Ibid.

18. Salvador de Madariaga, *Hernán Cortés: Conqueror of Mexico*, Garden City, NY: Doubleday, 1969, pp. 291–292.

19. Jon Ewbank Manchip White, *Cortés and the Downfall of the Aztec Empire*, New York: St. Martin's Press, 1971, pp. 212–213.

Chapter 8
Aztec Uprising

20. Ibid., p. 220.

21. Ibid., p. 226.

22. Ibid., 228.

Chapter 9
Conquest!

23. Francisco Lopez de Gomara, *Cortés: The Life of the Conqueror by His Secretary*, Berkeley: University of California Press, 1964, p. 253.

24. Jon Ewbank Manchip White, *Cortés and the Downfall of the Aztec Empire*, New York: St. Martin's Press, 1971, p. 244.

25. Ibid., 250.

26. Ibid., 259.

27. Ibid., 260

Chapter 10
"I Am the Man!"

28. Salvador de Madariaga, *Hernán Cortés: Conqueror of Mexico*, Garden City, NY: Doubleday, 1969, p. 438.

29. Jon Ewbank Manchip White, *Cortés and the Downfall of the Aztec Empire*, New York: St. Martin's Press, 1971, p. 295.

Blacker, Irwin R. *Cortés and the Aztec Conquest.* New York: American Heritage Publishing Company, 1965.

Diaz del Castillo, Bernal. *The True History of the Conquest of Mexico.* Ann Arbor, MI: University Microfilms, 1966.

Lopez de Gomara, Francisco. *Cortés: The Life of the Conqueror by His Secretary.* Berkeley, CA: University of California Press, 1964.

Madariaga, Salvador de. *Hernán Cortés: Conqueror of Mexico.* Garden City, NY: Doubleday, 1969.

Marrin, Albert. *Aztecs and Spaniards.* New York: Atheneum, 1986.

Prescott, William Hickling. *History of the Conquest of Mexico, and the History of the Conquest of Peru.* New York: The Modern Library, 1936.

Thomas, Hugh. *Conquest: Montezuma, Cortés, and the Fall of Old Mexico.* New York: Simon & Schuster, 1993.

White, Jon Ewbank Manchip. *Cortés and the Downfall of the Aztec Empire.* New York: St. Martin's Press, 1971

Books

Cortés, Hernán. *Letters From Mexico*. New Haven, CT: Yale University Press: 2001.

De Angelis, Gina. *Hernándo Cortés and the Conquest of Mexico*. Philadelphia, PA: Chelsea House Publishers, 2000.

Flowers, Charles. *Cortés and the Conquest of the Aztec Empire in World History*. Berkeley Heights, NJ: Enslow, 2001.

Petrie, Kristin. *Hernan Cortés*. Minneapolis, MN: Abdo Publishing Company: 2004.

Ramen, Fred. *Hernán Cortés: The Conquest of Mexico and the Aztec Empire*. New York: Rosen Publishing Group, 2003.

Webites

Hernándo Cortés
http://www.cdli.ca/CITE/excortes.htm

Hernándo Cortés on the Web
http://www.isidore-of-seville.com/cortes/

The Fall of the Aztecs
http://www.pbs.org/conquistadors/cortes/cortes_flat.html

Hernán Cortés
http://cybersleuth-kids.com/sleuth/History/Explorers/Hernan_Cortes/

Rachel A. Koestler-Grack has worked with nonfiction books as an editor and writer since 1999. She lives on a hobby farm near Glencoe, Minnesota. During her career, she has worked extensively on historical topics, including the colonial era, the Civil War era, the Great Depression, and the civil rights movement.

William H. Goetzmann is the Jack S. Blanton, Sr. Chair in History and American Studies at the University of Texas, Austin. Dr. Goetzmann was awarded the Joseph Pulitzer and Francis Parkman Prizes for American History, 1967, for *Exploration and Empire: The Explorer and the Scientist in the Winning of the American West.* In 1999, he was elected a member of the American Philosophical Society, founded by Benjamin Franklin in 1743, to honor achievement in the sciences and humanities.